EYEWITNESS
DINOSAUR

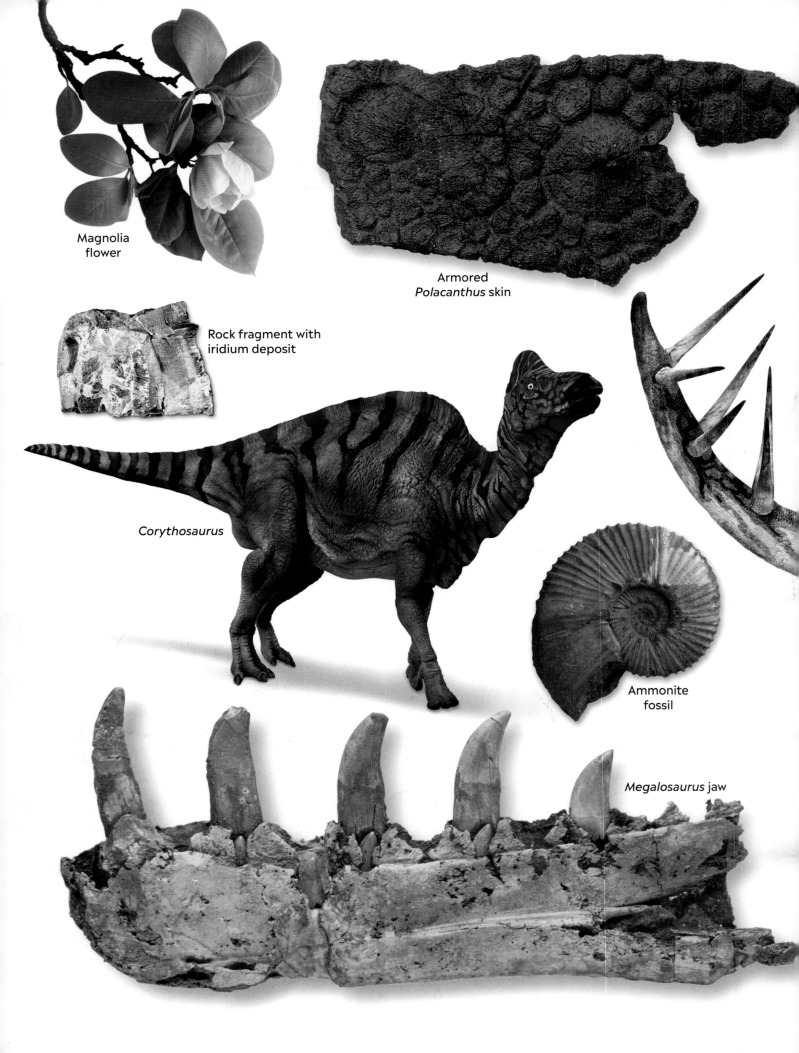

Magnolia
flower

Armored
Polacanthus skin

Rock fragment with
iridium deposit

Corythosaurus

Ammonite
fossil

Megalosaurus jaw

EYEWITNESS
DINOSAUR

AUTHOR **DAVID LAMBERT**

Kentrosaurus

Ammonite
mold

Ammonite
cast

Gila monster

DK | Penguin
Random
House

REVISED EDITION

DK LONDON
Senior Editor Carron Brown
Senior Art Editor Lynne Moulding
US Editor Megan Douglass
US Executive Editor Lori Cates Hand
Managing Editor Francesca Baines
Managing Art Editor Philip Letsu
Production Editor George Nimmo
Production Controller Samantha Cross
Jacket Design Development Manager Sophia MTT
Publisher Andrew Macintyre
Associate Publishing Director Liz Wheeler
Art Director Karen Self
Publishing Director Jonathan Metcalf

Consultant Chris Barker

DK DELHI
Senior Editor Shatarupa Chaudhuri
Senior Art Editor Vikas Chauhan
Art Editors Baibhav Parida, Sanya Jain
Assistant Editor Sai Prasanna
Senior Picture Researcher Surya Sankash Sarangi
Managing Editor Kingshuk Ghoshal
Managing Art Editor Govind Mittal
Senior DTP Designer Neeraj Bhatia
DTP Designer Pawan Kumar
Jacket Designer Juhi Sheth

FIRST EDITION
DK LONDON
Consultant Dr. David Norman
Senior Editor Rob Houston
Editorial Assistant Jessamy Wood
Managing Editors Julie Ferris, Jane Yorke
Managing Art Editor Owen Peyton Jones
Art Director Martin Wilson
Associate Publisher Andrew Macintyre
Picture Researcher Louise Thomas
Production Editor Melissa Latorre
Production Controller Charlotte Oliver
Jacket Designers Martin Wilson, Johanna Woolhead
Jacket Editor Adam Powley

DK DELHI
Editor Kingshuk Ghoshal
Designer Govind Mittal
DTP Designers Dheeraj Arora, Preetam Singh
Project Editor Suchismita Banerjee
Design Manager Romi Chakraborty
Production Manager Pankaj Sharma

This Eyewitness ® Guide has been conceived by
Dorling Kindersley Limited and Editions Gallimard

This American edition, 2021
First American edition, 1990
Published in the United States by DK Publishing
1450 Broadway, Suite 801, New York, NY 10018

A catalog record for this book is available from the Library of Congress.
ISBN: 978-0-7440-3908-5 (Paperback)
ISBN: 978-0-7440-3907-8 (ALB)

DK books are available at special discounts when purchased in bulk
for sales promotions, premiums, fund-raising, or educational use.
For details, contact: DK Publishing Special Markets,
1450 Broadway, Suite 801, New York, NY 10018
SpecialSales@dk.com

Printed and bound in China

For the curious
www.dk.com

Monolophosaurus

Iguanodon
hand

Ankylosaur
scute
(bony plate)

MIX
Paper from
responsible sources
FSC™ C018179

This book was made with Forest Stewardship Council™ certified
paper—one small step in DK's commitment to a sustainable future.
For more information go to www.dk.com/our-green-pledge

Oviraptor egg

Contents

Tyrannosaurus rex

6
The age of dinosaurs

8
Dinosaur types

10
Triassic times

12
Jurassic times

14
Cretaceous times

16
The end of an era

18
How do we know?

20
The first fossil finds

22
Little and large

24
Evolution

26
Heads and brains

28
Horns and crests

30
Senses

32
Meat-eaters

34
Plant-eaters

36
Long and short necks

38
The backbone story

40
All about tails

42
Terrifying tails

44
Plates and sails

46
Arms and hands

48
Claws and their uses

50
Legs and feet

52
Ancient footprints

54
Tough skins

56
Feathers

58
Eggs and young

60
Finding fossils

62
Rebuilding a dinosaur

64
Classifying dinosaurs

66
Discovery timeline

68
Find out more

70
Glossary

72
Index

The age of dinosaurs

Dinosaurs began to evolve 240 million years ago (mya) and ranged in size from gigantic, now extinct, reptiles to tiny modern hummingbirds. Only one dinosaur group survived the mass extinction 66 million years ago to live in the modern world—birds.

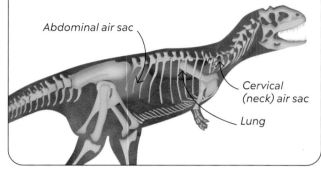
A TIME BEFORE HUMANS

Non-bird dinosaurs lived in the Mesozoic Era, about 252–66 million years ago (mya). This era is further divided into the Triassic, Jurassic, and Cretaceous periods. Other than birds, all dinosaurs died out long before the first humans appeared.

Modern humans appeared only around 300,000 years ago

"Age of dinosaurs"

252 mya	201 mya	145 mya	66 mya	today
Triassic	Jurassic	Cretaceous		
	MESOZOIC ERA		CENOZOIC ERA	

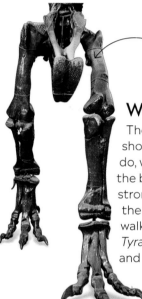

Head of thigh bone points inward to fit into the hip socket, which helps keep the limb erect

Walking tall

The limb bones of dinosaurs show that they walked as mammals do, with their legs underneath the body. The limbs had to be strong as some dinosaurs were the heaviest animals to ever walk on land. Like all dinosaurs, *Tyrannosaurus* walked on its toes, and had a hinge-like ankle joint.

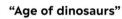

The **72 vertebrae** in *Elasmosaurus*'s **neck** made scientists initially mistake it for the reptile's tail.

Extremely long neck supported by 72 cervical vertebrae (neck bones)

Fossil feathers

The brown fringes around the skeleton of this fossil *Microraptor* are traces of feathers. Some dinosaurs had downy feathers for warmth; others had showy feathers to attract a mate. *Microraptor's* long feathers helped it glide between trees.

Opening in skull in front of eye reduced the weight of the skull

Neck with S-shaped curve

A hole in the lower jaw was inherited from ancient archosaur ancestors

Dinosaur features

Dinosaurs had many shared traits that help classify them. These include muscle attachment points on the neck bones and an open hip socket. Over the course of dinosaur evolution, some of these traits were lost or modified in certain groups. The Middle Jurassic predator *Monolophosaurus* retains many of the characteristics of the first dinosaurs, such as eating meat and walking on two legs.

Hand with three main digits

Weight-bearing toe

Terrible lizards?

Evidence suggests that dinosaurs were warm-blooded. Modern reptiles, such as this iguana lizard, are cold-blooded, which means they rely on the sun's heat for body warmth.

Green, scaly skin

Sprawling leg

Enormous, rigid flipper

Reptile relations

During the Mesozoic Era, the seas were ruled by large non-dinosaur reptiles, such as the plesiosaurs, mosasaurs, and ichthyosaurs. *Elasmosaurus* was the longest-known plesiosaur, growing to lengths of up to 33 ft (10 m).

Flipper-shaped limb

Dinosaur types

Scientists usually divide dinosaurs into two groups according to how their hip bones are arranged. The saurischians included the plant-eating sauropods and the meat-eating theropods. The ornithischians were mainly plant-eaters and included the ornithopods, as well as the plated, armored, and horned dinosaurs. The family tree on pages 64–65 shows how all these dinosaurs were related.

Heavy tail

Hip bones face in different directions

Hip bones lie next to each other

Psittacosaurus, an ornithischians

Eoraptor, a saurischian

Marginocephalians

Two major groups made up the marginocephalians: the horned and frilled ceratopsians, and the dome-head pachycephalosaurs. Ceratopsians were large herbivores, while pachycephalosaurs were smaller and may have been omnivores, eating both plants and meat.

A hip issue

Saurischians and ornithischians can be split based on the shape of their hip bones. In saurischians, one of the hip bones called the pubis points forward. However, in some saurischians, such as several theropods and birds, the pubis evolved to point backward. This orientation of the pubis also evolved in the ornithischians, in which all the hip bones pointed backward.

Bony plate

Stegosaurus, a stegosaur

Pentaceratops, a ceratopsian

Thyreophorans

This group included the stegosaurs and ankylosaurs, as well as some close relatives. Armor in the form of osteoderms protruded from the skin in all thyreophorans.

Large snout may have been used in display

Ornithopods

Some of these herbivores had showy crests for display, and hundreds of plant-crushing teeth. Evidence suggests ornithopods were social and formed herds.

Muttaburrasaurus,
an ornithopod

Immensely long neck

Air-filled spaces in the bones helped lighten the skeletons of giant sauropods

Scientists have found fossils of more than
800
different species
of dinosaur.

Bony spike jutting from skull

Bony neck frill

Short, sharp horn on the snout

Brachiosaurus,
a sauropod

Sauropodomorphs

Although early species were bipedal—they walked on two legs—most members of this group walked on four legs and had a distinctive long neck. One subgroup, the sauropods, evolved into the largest animals to ever walk the planet.

Cutting beak

Theropods

The dinosaurs that would eventually give rise to birds were bipedal. Many theropods were predators and ate meat, but some evolved plant-based diets.

Bulky neck muscles helped tear flesh and bone from carcasses

Tyrannosaurus rex,
a theropod

9

Ancient plants

Plants thrived where the soil was moist. Bushy-topped *Pleuromeia* was a short, unbranched, treelike plant that grew near coasts and river valleys. Damp places were also home to ferns and horsetails. Drier regions suited plants, including ginkgoes, ferns, cycads, and tall conifers related to the monkey puzzle tree.

Grasslike leaves on a single trunk

Pleuromeia plants

Desertlike region

Triassic times

The Triassic Period lasted from around 252 to 201 million years ago (mya). Life was recovering from the world's most devastating mass extinction, and conditions were harsh. Great deserts covered much of Earth, and there was less oxygen in the air than today. Dinosaurs evolved early on in the Triassic, but the first ones were small and rare compared to other animals.

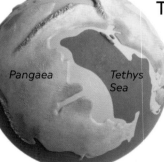

The Triassic world

In this period, Earth's continents were joined as a single landmass called Pangaea. Surrounding this landmass was a single ocean, with a great inlet called the Tethys Sea.

Pangaea

Tethys Sea

Leaves of a ginkgo tree

Fur probably covered body

Mammal-like teeth of different shapes and sizes

Mammals

During the Triassic Period, the closest relatives of mammals evolved. The small, shrewlike *Megazostrodon* lived in southern Africa and had almost all the features of a mammal. It would have snapped up insects and lizards, but kept well away from hungry dinosaurs.

Fern frond

Sea reptiles

Placodus ("flat tooth") was as long as a man and belonged to a group of sea reptiles called placodonts. About 240 million years ago, this bulky, short-necked creature plucked shellfish from rocks with its jutting front teeth, then crushed them using flat teeth in the roof of its mouth.

Armored back

Front teeth project forward

Sprawling limb

Beaklike snout cropped plants

Fossil skull

Plant-eating reptiles

Several groups of giant reptiles dominated Triassic wildlife before dinosaurs replaced them. This beaked skull comes from *Hyperodapedon*, a piglike reptile that belonged to a group of plant-eating reptiles called rhynchosaurs.

Wing membrane

Clawed finger

Flexible neck

Pseudosuchians

These animals formed one group of the ancient reptiles called archosaurs. Closely related to modern crocodilians, they flourished during the Triassic. All except one line died before the Jurassic. Scientists concluded that the lone survivors spread and eventually evolved into alligators and crocodiles.

Prestosuchus,
a pseudosuchian

Reptiles take flight

Eudimorphodon was a flying reptile about 28 in (70 cm) long. It was one of the earliest-known pterosaurs, which were flying relatives of dinosaurs. It had wings made of skin, a long, bony tail, and toothy jaws that could seize small fish.

Dawn of the dinosaurs

The first dinosaurs were probably small meat-eaters that were bipedal (walking on two legs). Plant-eaters, both bipedal and quadrupedal (walking on all fours), appeared at the end of the Triassic Period.

Herrerasaurus (231 mya)
This bipedal hunter from Argentina is one of the earliest-known dinosaurs. It used its long tail for balance when running.

Plateosaurus (210 mya)
This European "prosauropod" grew to 26 ft (8 m) long, but the bulky plant-eater supported itself on its hind limbs only.

Coelophysis (212 mya)
This theropod had slim, pointed jaws and swallowed smaller creatures. It is known from hundreds of individual skeletons.

Agile fliers

Many Jurassic pterosaurs, such as *Pterodactylus*, were larger than their Triassic ancestors. Shorter tails and flamboyant head crests were new features seen during this time. While they dominated the skies, they had to begin sharing their aerial domain with a new type of Jurassic animal—birds.

Long neck

Wing made of skin

Cycad-like leaves

Jurassic times

The Jurassic Period lasted from around 201 to 145 million years ago (mya). By now the continent Pangaea had begun to break into two large landmasses and the Atlantic Ocean had begun to form. Moist ocean winds brought rain to deserts. It was warm everywhere. Plants began to grow in barren lands, providing food for new kinds of dinosaur. Pterosaurs shared the skies with the first birds. Early salamanders swam in lakes and streams, and Jurassic seas swarmed with big, swimming reptiles.

Laurasia
Laurasia
Laurasia
Atlantic Ocean
Tethys Sea
Gondwana

The Jurassic world

Pangaea broke up into two landmasses called Laurasia and Gondwana. The North Atlantic also began to form during this time, but remained a narrow slither of sea for much of the Jurassic. No ice caps were present, and sea levels changed throughout the period.

Giants and birds

During the Jurassic Period, the "prosauropods" died out, but sauropods and theropods flourished. The ornithopods, stegosaurs, and ankylosaurs all appeared in this period.

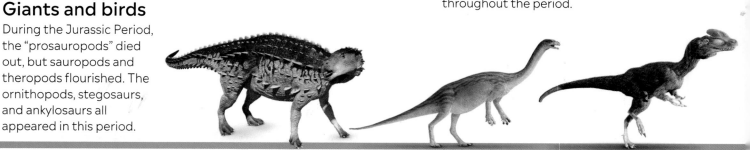

Scelidosaurus (190 mya)
The ankylosaur *Scelidosaurus* lived in Europe and was one of the earliest and most primitive armored dinosaurs.

Anchisaurus (190 mya)
The sauropod *Anchisaurus* ("near lizard") inhabited North America. This herbivore had ridged teeth that could shred leaves.

Guanlong (160 mya)
Guanlong belonged to the tyrannosauroid group of theropods. This crested dinosaur from China grew only 10 ft (3 m) long.

Jurassic vegetation

The major Jurassic plants were those that had flourished in the Triassic Period. These included ginkgoes, monkey puzzle trees, and cycadeoids, such as *Williamsonia*—a small, stumpy tree with palmlike leaves. Ferns, horsetails, and mosses thrived in areas with damp soil.

Williamsonia plants

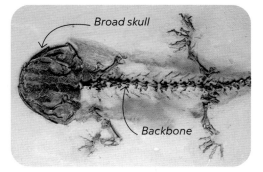

Leaves of a monkey puzzle tree

Crocodile ancestor

Protosuchus ("first crocodile") belonged to the same group of reptiles as modern crocodiles and alligators. It had longer legs and ran around on land. It was the size of a large dog and lived in Arizona.

Short jaws

Jurassic sea reptiles

Apart from a vertical tail, *Ichthyosaurus* was shaped like a dolphin. It grew 6½ ft (2 m) long and swam at speed. Ichthyosaurs were one of several groups of large Jurassic sea reptiles that were not related to dinosaurs.

Broad skull

Backbone

First salamanders

Frogs and salamanders as we know them today first appeared in the Jurassic Period. *Karaurus* is one of the earliest-known salamanders. About 8 in (20 cm) long, this small amphibian was a good swimmer. It probably lived in streams and pools, snapping up snails and insects.

Kentrosaurus (153 mya)
Related to *Stegosaurus*, the African *Kentrosaurus* ("spiky lizard") had narrow plates jutting from its neck, back, and tail.

Sinraptor (155 mya)
Sinraptor lived in what is now a desert in northwest China. This big meat-eater grew to more than 25 ft (7.6 m) long.

Archaeopteryx (150 mya)
The crow-size bird *Archaeopteryx* had feathered wings and body but also had a theropod's teeth, claws, tail, and scaly legs.

The Cretaceous world

In the Cretaceous Period, Laurasia and Gondwana broke apart. Their fragments began taking on the shapes and positions of the continents we know today. For a while, shallow seas flowed over stretches of low-lying land.

Cretaceous times

Marking the end of the Mesozoic Era, the Cretaceous Period lasted from 145 to 66 million years ago (mya). Climates remained warm, but great changes took place. Flowering plants appeared, lands flooded, and continents moved apart. The late Cretaceous Period probably saw more kinds of dinosaur than ever before.

Wing making downstroke

Beak with small teeth

Here come the birds

The common ancestor of all living birds first evolved in the Cretaceous Period—however, more primitive types were still abundant. The starling-size *Jinguofortis* resembled a modern bird, but it had tiny teeth and clawed wings.

An age of diversity

Cretaceous dinosaurs included some of the most massive sauropods and theropods of all time. Theropods now also included an amazing variety of feathered birds and birdlike dinosaurs. Stegosaurs had vanished, but the horned dinosaurs appeared, as well as the largest ankylosaurs and ornithopods.

From foliage to flowers

In the early Cretaceous Period, plants such as conifers and ferns still covered the land. One plant of the time was the tree-fern *Tempskya*, which had a false trunk made of stems. Flowering plants and shrubs began to grow on open ground. These new plants provided different kinds of food for plant-eating dinosaurs.

Magnolia flower

Alxasaurus (117 mya)
Alxasaurus from China's Alxa Desert was an early therizinosauroid – one of a group of plant-eating theropods.

Sauropelta (110 mya)
Sauropelta was an ankylosaur that roamed North American woodlands. Bony cones and studs guarded its back and tail.

Airborne giant

The Cretaceous saw the evolution of the largest flying animals ever to exist. *Quetzalcoatlus* had a wingspan of 39 ft (12 m), but it likely spent a lot of time on the ground, stalking small prey like baby dinosaurs. It lived at the end of the Cretaceous, 66 million years ago.

Trailing foot

Immensely long wing

Sea monster

Measuring about 41 ft (12.5 m) long, *Mosasaurus* was one of the largest of the marine reptiles called mosasaurs in the late Cretaceous. Mosasaurs were related to lizards, with paddle-shape limbs; a long, flattened tail; and huge, sharp-toothed jaws.

Late Cretaceous landscape

Modern mammals

New kinds of mammal emerged in the Cretaceous Period, including *Zalambdalestes*, which had a long nose like that of an elephant shrew. It lived in late Cretaceous Mongolia and hunted in the undergrowth, crushing insects between molar teeth.

Lightweight, furry body

Long tail

Styracosaurus (76.5 mya)
A large horned dinosaur from North America, *Styracosaurus* had long spikes on its neck frill and a sharp beak.

Albertosaurus (70 mya)
A predator with a massive head and tiny, two-fingered hands, *Albertosaurus* was smaller than its relative *Tyrannosaurus*.

Saltasaurus (68 mya)
Named after Salta where its fossils were first found, this sauropod had bony lumps on its hide.

Edmontosaurus (66 mya)
Edmontosaurus was one of the last and largest of the hadrosaurs (duck-billed dinosaurs). It grew up to 43 ft (13 m) long.

The end of an era

Volcanic eruptions

It was thought large-scale volcanic eruptions, which were occurring around the time of the mass extinction, might have contributed to the dinosaurs' downfall. Scientists now know they were not large enough to cause the extinction, and may have actually reduced the severity of the disaster due to their climate warming effects.

Dinosaurs flourished during the Mesozoic for more than 170 million years. Then, about 66 million years ago, they all disappeared except for the small theropods that we know as birds. This mass extinction was caused by a catastrophic asteroid impact, which hit Earth with the force of several million atomic bombs.

Fireball striking Earth

Shockwave

Asteroid impact

About 66 million years ago, an asteroid measuring 6–9 miles (10–14 km) wide crashed into Earth at several thousand miles an hour. The impact ejected huge amounts of rock into the atmosphere, which burned up to produce soot. Up to 2.5 trillion tons of soot is estimated to have blanketed Earth, blocking out the sun and cooling the planet greatly. This led to the extinction of seven out of every ten species of creature that lived on land or at sea.

Satellite image of
Central America

Impact crater in
Mexico's Yucatán
Peninsula

Strongly
magnetic
rocks at
center

Iridium deposits

Scientists have found a layer of iridium, a rare
element on Earth, above the last rock layer with
fossil dinosaurs, and below the first rock layer
without dinosaur fossils. It is believed that this
iridium came from the asteroid that formed
the Chicxulub crater.

Chicxulub crater

A crater 112 miles (180 km) across
marks where the asteroid hit Earth.
Engineers discovered the crater when
searching for oil near Puerto
Chicxulub, Mexico. Scientists found a
concentration of magnetic rocks at the
crater's center, shown in red here. These
rocks were lifted from deep beneath
Earth's surface when the asteroid struck.

Map of the magnetic
field in the crater region

Tiny victims

Late in the Cretaceous
Period, the shells of trillions
of tiny organisms called
coccolithophores formed
thick layers of chalk
beneath the sea. Almost
all coccolithophores
mysteriously disappeared
around the same time as
the non-bird dinosaurs.

Fragment
of chalk

Ammonite shells had
a ridged structure

Death in the sea

Ammonites (sea creatures related to
squid) also became extinct around
the same time as most dinosaurs.

Massive beak

Outlasting the catastrophe

Survivors of the mass extinction included the
theropods called birds. Some evolved into forms
such as the flightless *Gastornis*. Taller than a
man, it had a powerful kick and a massive
beak. Birds like this flourished for a
time, but eventually, they
died out as well.

Stumpy wings

Tidal waves
rippling over
the ocean

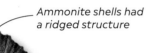

Hooflike
claws

Mammal survivors

About ten million years after the mass
extinction, mammals such as the plant-eater
Phenacodus had begun to appear. Mammals
survived the extinction as they were mainly
small, and could hibernate to avoid the
worst of the bad times.

Long, powerful
legs were
probably scaly,
like those of
modern birds

Limestone

Sandstone

Shale

Volcanic
ash

Limestone

Volcanic
ash

Shale

Limestone

How do we know?

Rock layers

Fossils occur in sedimentary rocks, which are formed when sand, mud, and gravel build up in layers over many millions of years. A series of rock layers can be seen in a cliff face (left). Index fossils are fossils that belong to a particular period, and help to date the rocks. Ammonites, for example, are index fossils for the Mesozoic Era.

We know what dinosaurs were like because paleontologists (scientists who study fossils) have dug up their remains. Fossils are the remains of plants and animals that have turned to rock over millions of years. Usually, only the more resistant parts are fossilized, such as bone or shell. However, occasionally soft tissue such as feathers, and evidence of pigments, are found.

Dinosaurs at river bank

Stack of layered rocks

Dry river bed

Digging up the past

Fossils need to be dug up according to local laws and guidelines. Determined dinosaur hunters often work in extremely harsh conditions to excavate fossil bones.

Prehistoric treasure

Almost all the bones in this *Heterodontosaurus* skeleton are still intact and most are connected to each other. Fossil dinosaur skeletons as complete as this are extremely rare. Dinosaur hunters are more likely to find tiny, isolated scraps of bone that were scattered by scavenging animals or the weather.

The story of a fossil

These block diagrams tell the story of dinosaurs that drowned in a river. Their bones were buried in layers of mud that slowly turned into rock. Minerals seeping into pores in the bones changed them into fossils. Over millions of years, wind and rain wore away the rocks, leaving the fossils exposed.

Trace fossils

A footprint shows where a dinosaur once walked through mud that later hardened into rock. Fossil eggs, nests, and dung also reveal how the living dinosaurs behaved. These fossilized signs, or traces, of an animal (rather than fossils of the animal itself) are known as trace fossils.

Dinosaur "mummy"

In 1908, fossil hunter Charles H. Sternberg and his three sons discovered a nearly intact dinosaur "mummy." This *Edmontosaurus* fossil was particularly special as it showed traces of pebbly skin. River mud covered the dead dinosaur before its body had decayed. A mold of the animal's skin was filled by mud that later turned to rock. This kind of preservation is extremely rare.

Fossilized skin impression covers fossil bones

Body contorts during decay process

"Mummified" *Edmontosaurus*

Impression of the organism

Stony lump in the shape of the organism

Frond-shaped carbon film

Ammonite mold

Ammonite cast

Molds and casts

Sometimes a dead organism rots away, leaving its impression in the mud. This kind of fossil is called a mold. As the mud turns into rock, minerals seep into the impression and form a stony lump in the shape of the organism. These fossils are called casts.

Carbonized plant

A shiny black and brown film made of carbon is all that remains of this fern frond preserved in a rock. Plant fossils help scientists to work out what the vegetation was like in a particular place at a particular time.

Bones of recently dead dinosaurs

Eroded desert

Layers building up on top

Dinosaur fossil

Paleontologist excavating a dinosaur fossil

The first fossil finds

In May 1821, Mary Mantell bought some unusual fossil teeth from a road worker, and gave them to her husband Gideon, a British paleontologist. He believed they came from a giant prehistoric reptile, which he named *Iguanodon*. British scientist Richard Owen realized *Iguanodon*, as well as two other large fossil reptiles, belonged to a single group that he called the Dinosauria, meaning "terrible lizards."

An early find

The first picture of a dinosaur fossil was published in 1677 in a book by Robert Plot, an English museum curator. Plot mistook the fossil for a thigh bone of a giant man.

Ridged teeth helped grind vegetation

A toothy clue

Gideon Mantell (1790–1852) noticed that large fossil teeth like this one resembled the smaller teeth of an iguana lizard. So he used the name *Iguanodon*, meaning "iguana toothed." Mary Mantell was actively involved in Gideon's work, drawing many of the specimens he studied.

Guess again!

Mantell's sketch shows what he believed *Iguanodon* looked like. It was largely guesswork based on a few broken bones. The animal resembles a large iguana lizard. Mantell mistook a thumb spike for a horn on its nose and he assumed its tail was whiplike, rather than heavy and stiff.

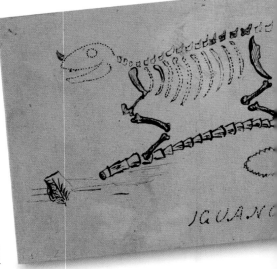

IGUANO

The first of many

In 1824, British geologist William Buckland (1784–1856) published his description of the *Megalosaurus* fossil. This was the first dinosaur to get a scientific name. Although Mantell named *Iguanodon* before Buckland printed the description of *Megalosaurus*, its name wasn't published until 1825.

Dentary (bone in lower jaw)

Megalosaurus jaw

Replacement tooth

What's in a name?

This cartoon is of Richard Owen (1804–1892), an expert in anatomy who coined the term "dinosaur." Owen realized that dinosaurs formed a special group because, unlike ordinary reptiles, they stood on erect limbs, and their backbones above the hips were fused (joined) together.

Life-size s...

The earliest life-size models resembled scaly, reptilian rh... Advised by Richard Owen, sculptor Waterhouse Hawkins made concrete of *Iguanodon* (below), *Megalos...* and *Hylaeosaurus*, and unveiled the... in an artificial lake in Crystal Palace Park in London, UK, in 1854.

Sharp, serrated tooth

Wild, wild west

In the 1870s, paleontologists discovered dinosaur fossils in quarries in the American Wild West. Famous US dinosaur hunter Barnum Brown (1873–1963) found the first *Tyrannosaurus* skeleton in Montana in 1902. He is pictured here with his wife at a quarry in 1941.

The forgotten dinosaur

Hylaeosaurus was an early Cretaceous ankylosaur, and was one of the three founding members included in Owen's "Dinosauria." Mantell officially named this heavily armored dinosaur *Hylaeosaurus* in 1833. This spiky herbivore was originally imagined as an overgrown lizard.

An artist's impression of *Hylaeosaurus*

and large

sculptures
of dinosaurs
inoceroses.
Benjamin
models
aurus,

'inosaurs as giant beasts, r than an elephant. auropods were the largest ever to walk on land. Built like a giant giraffe, *Brachiosaurus* stood as high as a four-story building. *Diplodocus* grew up to 110 ft (33.5 m). Single bones that have been found hint to the existence of even bigger sauropods, but working out their true size is a tricky task. In contrast, the theropod *Compsognathus* was little bigger than a chicken, and the tiny *Epidexipteryx* was smaller still.

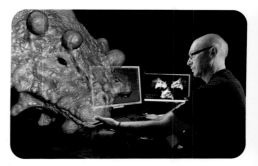

Calculating size

While measuring length or height is a straightforward job in dinosaurs with complete fossils, calculating how much they weighed is far trickier. Paleontologists sometimes create 3D computer models to estimate a dinosaur's volume, from which its weight can be calculated.

Extreme sizes

The head-to-tail lengths of these dinosaurs are compared to the height of a human being. Giants included the sauropod *Argentinosaurus* and the theropod *Carcharodontosaurus,* which dwarfed *Mei long*, its tiny relation. *Iguanodon* was one of the larger ornithopods, and *Triceratops* was among the largest horned dinosaurs.

Powerful hind limb

Sharklike teeth in a massive jaw

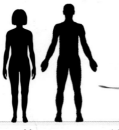

| Human 6 ft (1.8 m) | *Mei long* 27 in (68.5 cm) | *Carcharodontosaurus* 44 ft (13.5 m) | *Argentinosaurus* 100–110 ft (30.5–33.5 m) |

The high life
US paleontologist Earl Douglass found a large part of this specimen of *Barosaurus* in 1923. Although parts of the skeleton were kept at different museums, all of them were brought to the American Museum of Natural History (AMNH) in 1929. The mounted *Barosaurus* skeleton gives an idea of the creature's awesome size. Its head is 50 ft (15.2 m) above the ground.

Long neck

Small head relative to body size

Clawed finger

Dinosaur biplane
One of the smallest non-bird dinosaurs, *Microraptor* was about 30 in (77 cm) long and weighed only 2.2 lb (1 kg). According to some studies, this little theropod might have been capable of flying.

Feathered legs served as extra wings

Chicken-size
Compsognathus was once known as the smallest dinosaur. Scientists discovered that it preyed on lizards when they found the remains of the lizard *Schoenesmahl* in the rib cage of a fossilized *Compsognathus*.

Compsognathus

Chicken

Birdlike foot

Head could be lifted to about 16½ ft (5 m) above ground when rearing

Iguanodon
36 ft (11 m)

Triceratops
29½ ft (9 m)

Although it had a long and slender body, its head was flat and wide

Evolution

Both dinosaurs and humans evolved from the same prehistoric backboned animal. Evolution is a gradual process. Random differences in a population of organisms are passed on to their offspring. Beneficial differences that let organisms adapt successfully to their environment are more likely to be passed on. Over several generations, new species may form.

Fishy forerunner

Panderichthys was a fish that lived about 380 million years ago. A fish like this was the ancestor of all tetrapods (four-legged, backboned animals). Its fins were supported by bones like those found in our limbs, and its skull was similar in shape to those of early tetrapods.

Paddle-like tail fin

Eight digits

Not quite a tetrapod

Acanthostega was a close relative of tetrapods, in between its fishy ancestors and true tetrapods. It retained fishlike gills and its limbs were unable to support its weight on land. Instead, it likely lived in shallow water, hunting prey at the surface.

Lizard-like tail

Eggs with shells

The eggs of early tetrapods needed to be laid in water to prevent them from drying out. A group of tetrapods, called amniotes, evolved a new way of reproducing. They laid eggs with shells and complex tissues, which didn't dry out and could be laid away from water. These early amniotes eventually gave rise to mammals and reptiles (including birds).

Sprawling leg

A sprawling walker

Proterosuchus was a close cousin to a group of reptiles called archosaurs, which gave rise to crocodiles and dinosaurs. With limbs that stuck out sideways, *Proterosuchus* walked in a sprawling way.

Leg tucked in

Rearing to run

Agile archosaur cousins, such as the cat-size *Euparkeria*, were the descendants of the early, sprawling reptiles. *Euparkeria* lived about 245 million years ago. It walked on all fours, but may have reared to run on its hind limbs, using its tail for balance.

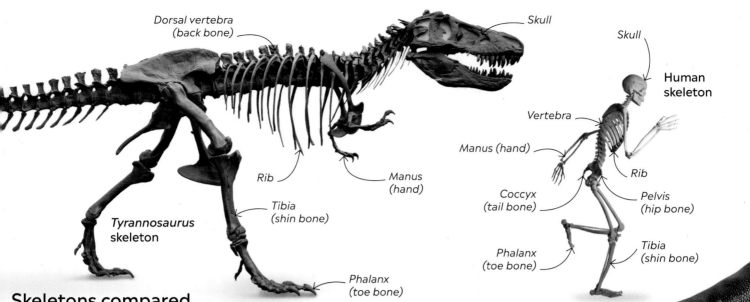

Skull

Human
skeleton

Skull

Dorsal vertebra
(back bone)

Vertebra

Manus (hand)

Rib

Rib

Manus
(hand)

Coccyx
(tail bone)

Pelvis
(hip bone)

Tibia
(shin bone)

Phalanx
(toe bone)

Tibia
(shin bone)

Tyrannosaurus
skeleton

Phalanx
(toe bone)

Skeletons compared

Tyrannosaurus and humans have a number of bones in
common, as they evolved from the same ancestor. The
main difference is in the number and proportion of some
bones. *Tyrannosaurus* has a longer skull. The dinosaur has
enough vertebrae to form a long tail, while humans
have one tail bone, known as the coccyx.

Dino dawn

One of the earliest dinosaurs was
Eoraptor, which lived 228 million
years ago. *Eoraptor*'s position in
the dinosaur family tree has been
heavily debated. Despite looking
like a theropod, it has sometimes
been grouped alongside early
sauropodomorphs. Scientists are not
certain of where to place *Eoraptor* as
it is very old and it shares traits with
dinosaurs in several different groups.

Heads and brains

A dinosaur's skull was made up of separate bones that slotted together to support the jaws and protect the brain. There were holes for eyes, nostrils, and jaw muscles, and often extra holes to save weight. Dinosaur brains were relatively smaller and less complex than those of most mammals. Some theropods had brains as large as those in certain modern birds. These dinosaurs probably had very keen senses.

Naris (opening for nostril)

Ankylosaurus

Armored head

Plant-eater *Ankylosaurus* was vulnerable to attacks by theropods. But this dinosaur had a thick, heavy, solid skull that protected its broad head from bites. There were no windows in its skull like those in many other dinosaurs. The only openings were four small holes for the eyes and nostrils.

Orbit (opening for eye)

Ankylosaurus skull

Naris (opening for nostril)

Camarasaurus

Slender rod of bone

Window

A skull with struts

The skulls of some dinosaurs were delicately built with slender rods of bone. This weight-saving design can be seen in the skull of the sauropod *Camarasaurus*. Strong muscles made this skull strong enough to withstand the force of a bite.

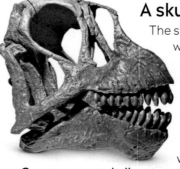

Camarasaurus skull

Antorbital fenestra
(window in front of
eye opening)

Tiny cerebrum

Brain
cast

Comparing brains

Tyrannosaurus's skull was much bigger
than a human skull, but compared with
ours, its brain was relatively small. A
brain cast showed that *T rex* had only
a tiny cerebrum—the part that makes
up most of the human brain. Our large
cerebrum makes complex thoughts
possible. With a simpler lifestyle than
our own, *T rex* managed very well with
a brain that mainly controlled the
muscles and the senses.

Cerebrum forms
85 percent of the
human brain

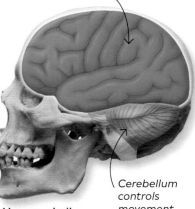

Cerebellum
controls
movement

Human skull

***Tyrannosaurus* skull**

Sweat around the
nose and mouth
evaporated with
the body's heat,
cooling the surface
as well as the blood
flowing to the brain

Quick-witted?

Following the extinction
of the non-bird dinosaurs,
some birds began
evolving bigger brains
relative to their body
size. Modern crows are
intelligent creatures,
and their brains contain
a similar number of cells
compared to the brains of
primates such as humans.

***Diplodocus,* a sauropod**

Keeping cool

Giant sauropods and
ankylosaurs were in danger of
overheating, so had large blood
vessels in the snout to help
shed excess heat. In theropods,
the big hole in the skull in front
of the eyes contained a large
sinus (air pocket). When the jaw
muscles moved, air could be
pumped in and out of this sinus,
helping shed excess heat.

Horn jutting from above the eyes

Bull's horns

Two cowlike horns stuck out sideways from the head of *Carnotaurus*. These horns were too short and stubby to help this theropod kill its prey and might have served as an ornament to attract a mate. However, a pair of dueling males could have used their horns as weapons, by shoving each other with their skulls.

Short snout

Three-horned face

Two brow horns 3.3 ft (1 m) long and a short nose horn earned *Triceratops* its name, which means "three-horned face." Some fossils show healed injuries to the frill where rival *Triceratops* gouged each other as they locked horns over mates. Other ceratopsians, such as *Centrosaurus*, typically show fewer head injuries, suggesting their headgear had more of a display role.

Long brow horn

Short nose horn

Horns and crests

The skulls of many dinosaurs had bumps, horns, or head crests. These likely had multiple uses. While some dinosaurs fought with these showy features, their main use was probably for display. Whether they were used to attract a mate or scare an enemy, extravagant headgear needed energy to grow and maintain.

Narrow beak

Nasal boss

A thick nose

Instead of the conical nose horn of most large plant-eating ceratopsians, the North American *Pachyrhinosaurus* ("thick-nosed lizard") grew a bony lump that was broad and flattish. The bone texture suggests a thick, hard pad covered the nasal boss. Rivals probably used these bumps to push each other until the weaker one gave way.

Curious crest

Evolving in the early Jurassic in Antarctica, *Cryolophosaurus* was among the first big theropods. Its head was adorned with a thin, horizontal crest. Scientists think that the largest theropods often evolved head ornaments compared to smaller ones. They suggest that large body sizes and fancy headgear could have been important for communication.

Shield-shaped back of skull

Helmet-shaped skull roof

Thick-headed

Pachycephalosaurs ("thick-headed lizards") such as *Stegoceras* had very thick skull roofs. These domes were used to head-butt rivals as they competed over food or mates. Partially healed fractures and signs of infection on these domes show how risky this fighting might have been, and some likely died from their injuries.

The head crest changed shape as Lambeosaurus *grew*

Crested dinosaurs

Tall, narrow crests crowned the heads of some hadrosaurs (a type of ornithopod). *Lambeosaurus* had a tall, bonnet-shaped crest, and *Parasaurolophus* had a huge, long crest that grew much earlier in life compared to other hadrosaurs, and may have helped it make low noises.

Lambeosaurus

Backward-pointing crest

Parasaurolophus

The crest could measure up to twice the size of the head

29

Senses

Dinosaurs depended on sight, smell, taste, hearing, balance, and touch to find food and mates, and to detect danger. Powerful scanners can help reveal the brain and nerve passages hidden within the skull bones, giving paleontologists a relatively good idea about the structure of their sensory systems and how they worked. Comparing dinosaurs to modern animals helps us imagine their way of life.

Blood vessels and nerves passed through the canals

Touchy subject

Within the snouts of some dinosaurs, such as the hunter *Neovenator*, were branching canals that housed blood vessels and nerves. While not as sensitive as the snouts of crocodilians, dinosaurs may have used their snouts to touch their environment, perhaps even rubbing snouts during courtship.

Dinosaurs could hear low-frequency sounds through thick vegetation and over long distances.

Listening out

Like ears in modern reptiles and birds, dinosaur ears were small holes located on the side of the head. Dinosaurs likely made a map in their heads depending on where sound waves hit their skull, similar to how modern alligators and birds hear.

Ear of an iguana

Dino tongues

Dinosaur tongues rarely, if ever, fossilize. However, the throat bones they attach to sometimes do, helping scientists compare dinosaurs with living animals. Most dinosaurs could not move their tongues. However, some, such as the ankylosaurs, had powerful tongues to help them process tough plant food.

Sniffing it out

Tyrannosaurus ("tyrant lizard") had large olfactory lobes—parts of the brain that identify various smells. This suggests that this Cretaceous theropod had a keen sense of smell. Other theropods, such as *Gallimimus*, had small olfactory lobes, and scent was probably not important to its herbivorous diet.

Large eyes had good night vision

In the dark

A fossil of the small ornithischian *Leaellynasaura* suggested it had large eye sockets, a potentially useful adaptation to see in the long, dark winter nights near the South Pole. However, this specimen was a juvenile, and proportionally bigger eyes are traits often seen in young dinosaurs.

Dinosaurs likely had good color vision

Eyes forward

Tyrannosaurus rex had large, forward-facing eyes that could see and focus on the same thing at once, such as baby hadrosaur prey. The eyes produced a 3D image of the prey in *T rex*'s brain, and enabled the theropod to judge the distance between itself and its victim.

Side vision

Like a horse, the ostrichlike dinosaur *Gallimimus* had an eye on each side of its head—one looked left and the other looked right. Each eye saw things the other could not. Between them, the two eyes could spot a predator creeping up from behind. This gave *Gallimimus* time to dash away before being caught.

SEEING THINGS

The areas in blue show how much of the world *Gallimimus* and *T rex* could see. *Gallimimus* had a much wider field of vision than *T rex*, but *T rex* could judge distances better directly in front.

Field of vision of left eye

Narrow field of overlapping vision

Field of vision of right eye

Narrow field of overlapping vision

Field of vision of right eye

Field of vision of left eye

Gallimimus's field of vision

T rex's field of vision

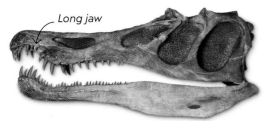

Long jaw

Versatile hunter

Baryonyx belonged to a group of unusual theropods called spinosaurids. Evidence suggests they spent a lot of time in or around water, and their diet included a range of prey, such as young dinosaurs, pterosaurs, and fish.

Bone fragments of prey

Dinosaur droppings

Scientists study the fossil droppings of large theropods to discover which animals they ate. They look for undigested scraps of bones and compare them with those of known types of dinosaur. This tyrannosaur dropping contains the remains of either a horned or a duck-billed dinosaur.

Meat-eaters

Many large meat-eating dinosaurs, such as *Tyrannosaurus*, had powerful jaws and knifelike teeth for killing and tearing up big prey. But not all theropods had heads for tackling such heavy tasks. Spinosaurids were shaped for seizing a range of different prey, including fish, and small, sharp-toothed coelurosaurs swallowed lizards whole. Ornithomimids were toothless and evolved beaks, allowing them to nip off vegetation.

Killing teeth

With serrated edges like a knife, the curved teeth of *Megalosaurus* sliced easily through flesh. Such use meant teeth were quickly worn or lost during feeding. This was not a problem as theropods replaced their teeth throughout their lives. *Allosaurus*'s teeth were replaced every 100 days or so, but in *Majungasaurus*, this happened every 56 days.

New tooth

Megalosaurus tooth

Triceratops

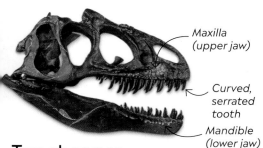

Maxilla
(upper jaw)

Curved,
serrated
tooth

Mandible
(lower jaw)

Top chopper

Sturdy bones in *Allosaurus*'s skull supported its jaw and bladelike teeth. The jaw joint acted like scissors. 3D computer analysis has shown that it tore off flesh like a living bird of prey, quickly jerking the head down and back to rip off a juicy morsel.

A toothless theropod

Citipati belongs to a group of theropods called oviraptorosaurs. Despite being theropods, which were mainly meat-eaters, later oviraptorosaurs had a toothless beak. A herbivorous lifestyle, with meat eaten from time to time, is probable.

Toothless beak

Citipati

Stomach

Gut and gizzard

A theropod's digestive juices dissolved meat. Meat has less fiber than plants, making it easier to digest than vegetation. This meant meat-eaters probably had shorter digestive tracks compared to herbivores.

Muscular back

Intestine

Tyrannosaur attack

This *Tyrannosaurus rex* is about to bite a *Triceratops*. Both dinosaurs lived in North America in the late Cretaceous Period. Although *Triceratops* was a large herbivore, the bone-crunching teeth and strong jaws of the larger *T rex* were adapted for taking down big game.

Tyrannosaurus

Balancing tail

OPEN WIDE

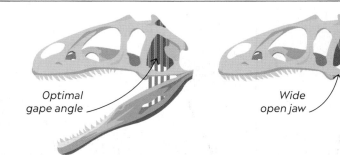

Optimal gape angle

Wide open jaw

Some predatory theropods, such as *Allosaurus*, could open jaws extremely wide. However, *Allosaurus* could bite most effectively when its jaws were more closely held together. Opening the jaws wide likely helped capture big prey.

Plant-eaters

The digestive systems of herbivorous dinosaurs were adapted for their plant-based diet. Sauropods stripped twigs with teeth shaped like spoons or pencils. Horned dinosaurs chewed tough vegetation with their sharp molars. Hadrosaurs crushed leaves using some of the most complex teeth in any animal. Most ornithischians probably had jaw muscle arrangements that acted like cheeks to hold food while chewing. All these dinosaurs likely had long intestines to digest plenty of plant food.

Stones in the gut
Smooth stones found in the remains of certain sauropods led some paleontologists to believe that they were used to grind food. Sauropods may have had a gizzard (muscular organ for grinding food) like a bird's. But scientists now think that the sauropods swallowed stones either by accident, or deliberately for their nourishing minerals.

Bendy neck allowed Diplodocus to feed over vast areas without walking too much

Mowing machine
Nigersaurus had more teeth than any other sauropod. Its lower jaw alone had 68 teeth. Behind each pencil-shaped front tooth, new teeth grew to replace lost teeth. With its square jaw, short-necked *Nigersaurus* cropped low-growing plants like a living lawnmower.

Many teeth in square jaw

Great grinder
Hadrosaurs, such as *Edmontosaurus*, had evolved complex teeth perfect for crushing plants. Instead of shedding teeth, old teeth were filled in with tough tissues in the mouth. With well over 1,000 teeth in the jaws, hadrosaurs could grind plants into an easily digested pulp.

Teeth held in jaw by ligaments

34

Three kinds of teeth

Heterodontosaurus was a small, early ornithischian with three kinds of teeth. Front teeth bit against a horny beak to snip off vegetation. Molars then mashed food into a pulp. Their "tusks," most paleontologists argue, would have been good for slicing vegetation, too.

Dentary (lower jaw bone)

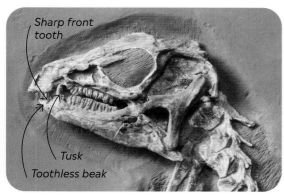

Sharp front tooth

Tusk

Toothless beak

Parrot beak

The name *Psittacosaurus* ("parrot lizard") was inspired by its parrotlike cutting beak. *Psittacosaurus* used its beak to slice off low-lying vegetation, although its boxy skull and deep jaw suggest perhaps tough food items, such as nuts, were also on the menu.

Wear and tear

Two *Iguanodon* molars—one new, one worn—show the effects of chewing tough plants. Each time *Iguanodon* closed its mouth to grind leaves, the two side rows of upper teeth slid across the surface of the lower teeth. This kept the teeth sharp but also wore them down.

Iguanodon teeth

Treetop browser

Measuring up to 108 ft (33 m) long, *Diplodocus* was one of the largest dinosaurs to have walked on Earth. *Diplodocus*'s pencil-shaped teeth were like rakes for stripping vegetation. This massive plant-eater ate up to 73 lb (33 kg) of ferns and leaves every day.

Diplodocus

Whiplike tail was made up of 80 bones

SAUROPOD DIGESTION

Leaves swallowed by a sauropod passed through its long intestines, where they were broken down into simple substances that could be carried around the body. Sauropods weren't fussy eaters, and bulk feeding on low-quality plants may have pushed them to all fours as their digestive tracts got bigger, but this is a difficult idea for scientists to test.

A mixed diet

Several distantly related herbivores, such as *Stegosaurus* and *Plateosaurus*, had remarkably similar skulls: narrow at the front, a downward-facing lower jaw, and a low jaw joint. However, computer analysis has shown that the skulls had different biting ability, probably reflecting different diets. A stronger bite helped *Stegosaurus* eat more types of plant.

Stegosaurus skull

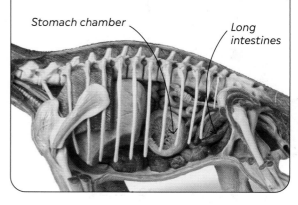

Stomach chamber

Long intestines

Braced for heady heights

Powerful neck muscles lifted *Brachiosaurus*'s head, and a strong heart pumped blood up to its brain. This sauropod's neck was supported at the base like a movable jib (arm) of a crane is supported by a tower and base. All sauropod necks were braced by muscles, tendons, and the cable-like ligament above the neck bones. Bracing strengthened the necks and made them flexible.

Crane with movable jib

Cervical vertebra (neck bone)

Mandible (lower jaw)

Long and short necks

Sauropods had the longest necks of all dinosaurs—some more than five times as long as a giraffe's. In contrast, most armored, plated, and horned dinosaurs had short, strong necks, and mostly fed on vegetation near the ground. Large meat-eaters, such as *Tyrannosaurus*, had massive necks, while smaller theropods, such as *Velociraptor*, had slim necks that uncoiled like springs when attacking prey.

Neck frill

Strong neck

Pentaceratops, a ceratopsid

Short and strong

In order to support their incredibly heavy skulls, the first three neck vertebrae were fused in ceratopsids, providing increased strength and stability.

Long neck may have helped it reach foliage 10 ft (3 m) off the ground

Labels along the top of the neck bones illustration:

- Hollowed-out areas lightened the neck bones
- Neural spine (ridge rising from vertebra)
- Joint between two vertebral centra (cores)
- Cervical rib for muscle attachment

Energy saver

Diplodocus's long neck was made up of light but strong hollowed-out bones. A large ligament ran along the top of the neck bones, and acted as an energy saving device, stopping the neck from sagging due to gravity while using very few muscles.

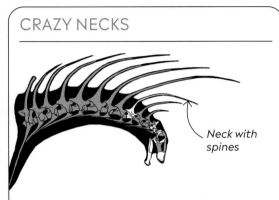

CRAZY NECKS

Neck with spines

Bajadasaurus had long, curved spikes jutting out of its neck. These might have been used in defense or for display and were probably covered in tough keratin—the same material as our fingernails.

Labels on Tyrannosaurus skeleton:

- Cervical vertebra
- Orbit (eye socket)
- Cervical rib
- Mandible

Tyrannosaurus skeleton

Powerful neck

Tyrannosaurus's huge head required a powerful neck to support it. Its small arms freed up space on the shoulder girdle for big neck muscles to attach, helping this predator control struggling prey and tear up carcasses.

Sauropod mimic

The unusual stegosaur *Miragaia* had a long neck made up of 17 bones—more than most sauropods! Its neck got longer by incorporating some of its back bones into it. It may have grown to impress mates, or gather more or different kinds of food compared to other dinosaurs.

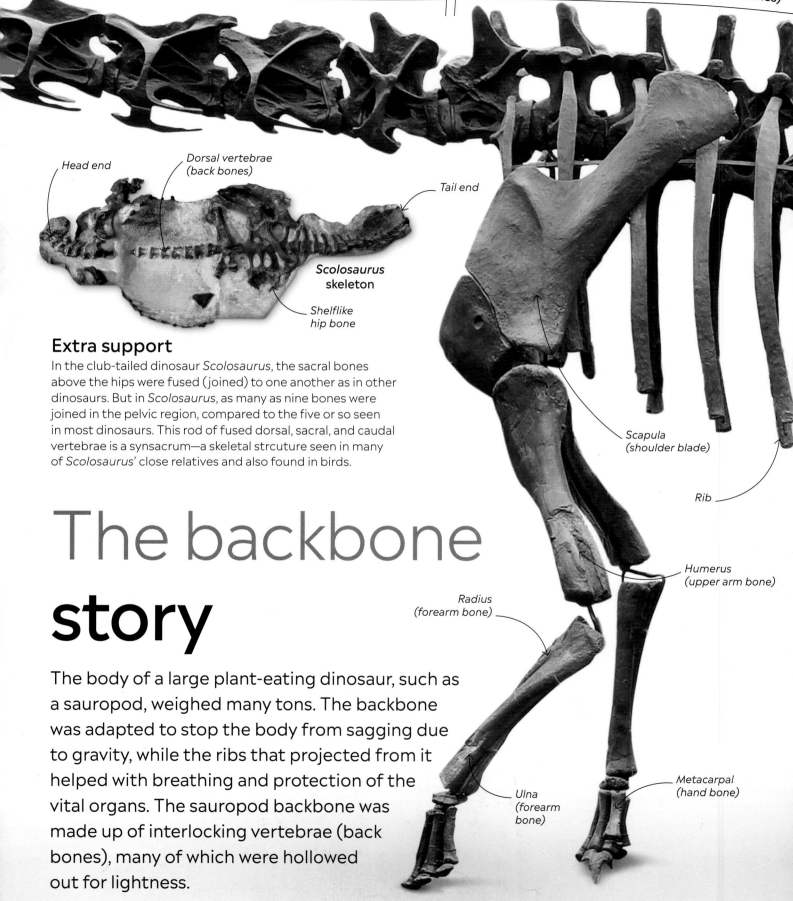

Cervical vertebrae (neck bones)

Dorsal vertebrae (back bones)

Head end

Dorsal vertebrae (back bones)

Tail end

Scolosaurus skeleton

Shelflike hip bone

Extra support

In the club-tailed dinosaur *Scolosaurus*, the sacral bones above the hips were fused (joined) to one another as in other dinosaurs. But in *Scolosaurus*, as many as nine bones were joined in the pelvic region, compared to the five or so seen in most dinosaurs. This rod of fused dorsal, sacral, and caudal vertebrae is a synsacrum—a skeletal strcuture seen in many of *Scolosaurus'* close relatives and also found in birds.

Scapula (shoulder blade)

Rib

The backbone story

The body of a large plant-eating dinosaur, such as a sauropod, weighed many tons. The backbone was adapted to stop the body from sagging due to gravity, while the ribs that projected from it helped with breathing and protection of the vital organs. The sauropod backbone was made up of interlocking vertebrae (back bones), many of which were hollowed out for lightness.

Humerus (upper arm bone)

Radius (forearm bone)

Metacarpal (hand bone)

Ulna (forearm bone)

Breakthrough bone

Found in the mid-1830s, this part of an *Iguanodon* backbone shows that the vertebrae between the hips were fused—something not seen in other reptiles. This was the clue that led scientists to realize that dinosaurs formed a whole new group of reptiles.

Sacral vertebrae (hip bones)

Caudal vertebrae (tail bones)

Ilium
(topmost
hip bone)

Spiny backbone

Narrow spines at the top of *Diplodocus*'s vertebrae provided anchor points for its powerful back muscles. These served to brace the center of the body during movement. In some dinosaurs, like *Spinosaurus* and *Ouranosaurus*, the spines became extremely long and likely had roles in display.

Ischium (lower,
rear hip bone)

Pubis (lower,
forward hip bone)

Femur (thigh bone)

Fibula (calf bone)

Tibia
(shin bone)

Metatarsal
(foot bone)

BIRD LUNGS

The backbones of saurischian dinosaurs had various holes, which contained extensions of the lung tissue called air sacs. These air sacs were even wedged into the hips and tails of certain species, and likely helped boost high-energy activities while also making the skeleton lighter.

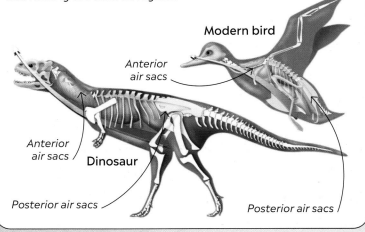

Modern bird

Anterior
air sacs

Anterior
air sacs

Dinosaur

Posterior air sacs

Posterior air sacs

All about tails

Dinosaur tails had many different uses. Most importantly, the tail helped dinosaurs move around. Front-heavy dinosaurs used their tails for balance as they walked or ran. Swift flicks of the tail allowed the dinosaur to change direction at speed. However, tails evolved to be more than just simple balancing aids.

*Caudal vertebra
(tail bone)*

*Chevrons become
increasingly small and fragile
near the end of the tail*

*Attachment area
for tail muscles*

*Elongated chevron
(V-shaped downward
projection of vertebra)*

*Back was held
horizontally
when running*

*Balancing
tail*

Balancing
on the move

All dinosaurs, including the ornithischian *Dryosaurus*, held their stiffened tail above the ground when walking, and held it out horizontally when running on its hind limbs. If chased, the dinosaur might have tried to escape by flicking its tail to one side, making a sudden, dodging turn to evade the predator.

*Strong leg muscles helped
Dryosaurus run fast*

*Tail provided balance
but its rigidity
hindered agility*

Tail bones of Nomingia,
an oviraptorosaur

*Fused vertebrae at
the end of the tail,
which held the fan
of feathers*

Feathered fan

Oviraptorosaur tails were short compared to their theropod cousins. A fan of feathers was a feature common to many of this group, and it is thought these flexible yet muscly tails may have been used as a display to attract mates.

**Tail stiffeners
in *Corythosaurus***

Caudal vertebra (tail bone)

Stiffening
tendon

Tails held high

Crisscrossing tendons stiffened the lower back
and upper tail of the hadrosaur *Corythosaurus*. Common
to most ornithischians, these bony tendons may have
helped stiffen the tail. As big leg muscles anchored into
the tail, having such a stable platform may have helped
them exert more power during locomotion.

Ischium
(hip bone)

Simple, rodlike
vertebra

Tail bones
become narrower
toward the end

Elongated tail

The core of *Diplodocus*'s tail was formed by 80
bones. At up to 43 ft (13 m), this sauropod's tail was
perhaps the longest of any dinosaur. When a herd of
Diplodocus walked together, the animals held their
tails high to counterbalance their necks.

Joint between
tail bones

Muscle power

Dinosaur hind legs were powered by
two huge muscles that ran along the
underside of the tail, each connected to
the back of a leg. They helped pull the leg
backward while moving. The theropod
Carnotaurus had particularly big muscles
along the tail, making it one of the fastest
large predators of the Mesozoic.

Terrifying tails

Turning the tail into a weapon by evolving clubs and spikes is a rare form of defense, but these features have been discovered across different dinosaur groups. In ankylosaurs and stegosaurs, such tail weapons were made of bony structures called osteoderms. Fossils of smaller clubs have been seen in certain older sauropods, too, and these potentially acted as mini-maces to hurt hungry theropods. Tail weapons appear to be mainly found in large, slow herbivores, which needed extra defenses against predators.

Cracking the whip

A lumbering sauropod's main defense was its sheer size and weight, but *Apatosaurus* and its relatives could also deliver stinging blows with their long, snaky tails. Some scientists have suggested that the elongate, thin tails of *Apatosaurus* and its relatives were used like a whip, to produce a thunderous crack to scare predators. The sheer weight of the tail could have caused a painful impact.

Cervical (neck) vertebrae

Apatosaurus skeleton

Ischium (hip bone)

Columnar leg

Flat head

Shunosaurus tail

Tail bones are slender, bony cylinders near tip of tail

Spikes were 2 in (5 cm) tall

Tall weapon

A slow-moving herbivore from 170 million years ago, *Shunosaurus* had a bony, clubbed tail. The tail club was lined with double rows of tall spikes called osteoderms, which might have been used to scare off Jurassic predators. Some experts have suggested that they could have been used for defense.

Lashing out

Crocodiles are the largest living reptiles to use their tails for defense. A dominant male may lash his tail from side to side to frighten off another male. Threatening displays like this are usually enough to drive off a rival—actual fights between males are rare.

Bony tail spike

Spiky tail

Kentrosaurus ("sharp point lizard") had many pairs of long spikes sticking out sideways and backward from its tail. The tail was flexible and could move in a wide, sweeping arch. If attacked by a predator, *Kentrosaurus* probably lashed out its tail using the spikes as swords to stab its attacker. All stegosaurs were armed with at least one pair of tail spikes like these.

Based on certain estimates, spikes on the tails of some stegosaurs were more than 3.3 ft (1 m) long.

Armored plates protected the body.

Ankylosaurus

ARMORED TAIL

Tail club

Ankylosaur tail clubs, like in this Ankylosaurus, were complex weapons. The huge bone clubs needed great amounts of energy to grow and keep healthy. While cracking theropod shins was a possible use, they may have had another function—to help while fighting one another. Injuries to the clubs have been found on several ankylosaurs, including fractures and infections from use.

Fossil of Ankylosaurus tail club

Plates and **sails**

Although rarely discovered, plates and sails evolved multiple times throughout history, including in several different dinosaurs. They are, however, made out of different bony structures. Plates are osteoderms (bony deposits) embedded in the skin, whereas sails are long processes (outgrowths) that develop from the vertebrae.

Artery brings hot blood into the plate to lose heat to the cool air

Vein takes cooled blood to the body

Heated debate

The role of Stegosaurus's plates in temperature control has been debated for several decades. Most paleontologists today consider these plates to be showy structures for display. An internal pipelike system of arteries and veins perhaps allowed for some heat loss. Their most likely main role, though, seems to be signaling.

Slender snout

Sail or ridge

Dorsal plate (plate on back)

Sail back

Spinosaurus ("spine lizard") was a huge theropod with a long snout. Spiny pieces of bone more than 6 ft (1.8 m) long jutted from its backbone like blades. Scientists don't know what it was used for, but given its large size, it may have been used for display.

Rib

Small skull

Cervical plate (neck plate)

Long hind limb

Short forelimb

Plated dinosaur

At about 29½ ft (9 m) long, *Stegosaurus* ("roof lizard") was the largest of all stegosaurs. Most stegosaurs sported two rows of tall spikes, but *Stegosaurus* had an alternating double row of plates along its neck, back, and tail. These structures have stirred quite a lot of debate, and some experts have even suggested they could move! However, this has not been proved.

Theropod oddball

Deinocheirus was a peculiar theropod, with enormous arms; a flat, duck-like snout; and deep lower jaw. It was a type of ornithomimosaur, and grew to enormous proportions. Adults may have grown to more than 36 ft (11 m), and a tall hump protruded from the back. Its use remains unknown.

Double spikes

The neck of the relatively short-necked sauropod *Amargasaurus* had paired rows of large spines jutting from the tops of the vertebrae. They were perhaps used in defense.

Double row of neural (backbone) spines

Largest plate

Caudal plate (plate on tail)

Caudal vertebra (tail bone)

Spine on caudal vertebra

Tall neural spine supported a sail or ridge

Ouranosaurus

Showy herbivore

Like *Spinosaurus*, display is the most likely explanation for the long processes on the back and tail of the ornithopod *Ouranosaurus*. The back muscles only attached to the base of the spines and there weren't many blood vessels, suggesting the sail was not used in temperature control.

Caudal spike (spike on tail)

"Armed" theropod

Deinocheirus ("terrible hand") had the longest arms of any known theropod. Each arm was longer than a human and ended in a three-fingered hand with large, curved claws. Scientists have suggested this giant ornithomimosaur's powerful yet peculiar arms hooked juicy plants out of lakes.

Humerus (upper arm bone)

Radius (forearm bone)

Phalanx (finger bone)

Ungual (claw)

Deinocheirus

Arms and hands

Dinosaurs' arms and hands evolved in remarkable ways. The first dinosaurs had flexible arms with five fingers on each hand to grasp and seize prey, but this pattern was modified in later dinosaur groups. Some theropods had long, gangly arms; others had tiny forelimbs. Plant-eaters, such as *Iguanodon*, used their hands for walking and grasping leaves. Sauropods' arms were weight-bearing props for their big, heavy bodies.

Skeleton of a pigeon

Extreme changes

The wings of modern birds evolved from the five digits and complex wrists of the earliest dinosaurs, representing one of the major evolutionary changes. The fingers and wrist bones fused to form wings. How the change occurred is still debated.

Humerus (upper arm)

Flexible fifth finger

Fourth finger

Third finger

Second finger

Made to multitask

Iguanodon had massive hands. The wrist bones were fused into a blocklike structure that, along with hooflike middle claws, helped support its huge body. The flexible fifth digit may have helped hold objects, while the function of the conical thumb spike remains a mystery.

Thumb spike bone

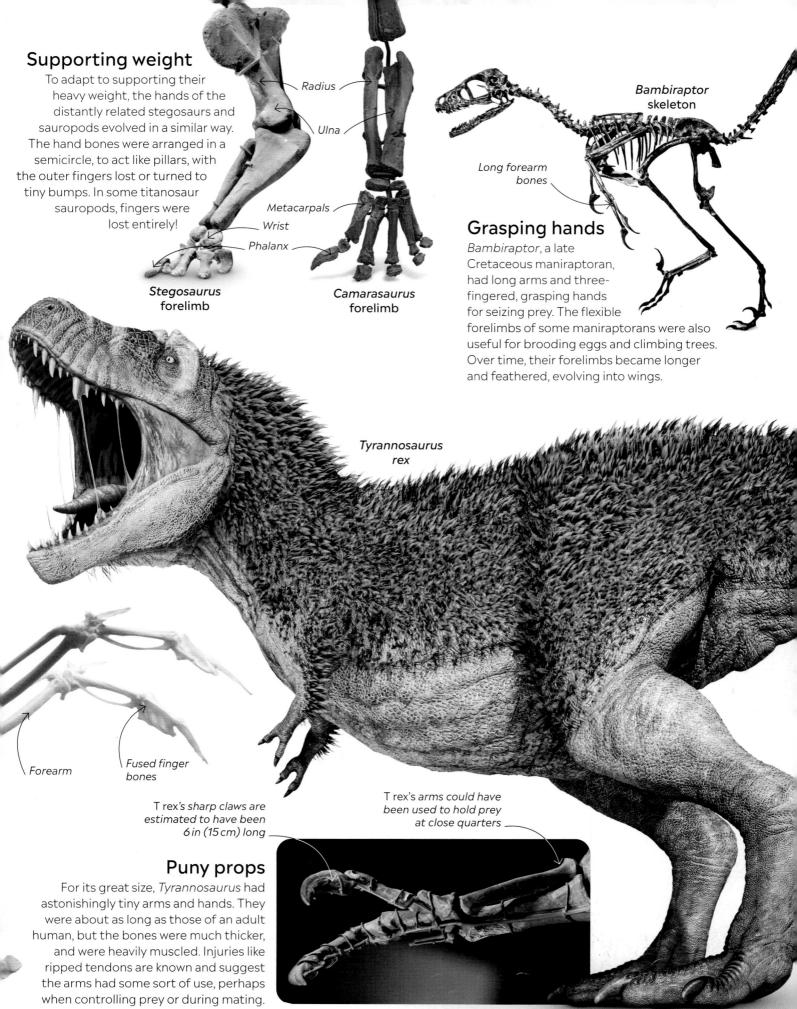

Supporting weight

To adapt to supporting their heavy weight, the hands of the distantly related stegosaurs and sauropods evolved in a similar way. The hand bones were arranged in a semicircle, to act like pillars, with the outer fingers lost or turned to tiny bumps. In some titanosaur sauropods, fingers were lost entirely!

Radius

Ulna

Metacarpals

Wrist

Phalanx

Stegosaurus
forelimb

Camarasaurus
forelimb

Bambiraptor
skeleton

Long forearm
bones

Grasping hands

Bambiraptor, a late Cretaceous maniraptoran, had long arms and three-fingered, grasping hands for seizing prey. The flexible forelimbs of some maniraptorans were also useful for brooding eggs and climbing trees. Over time, their forelimbs became longer and feathered, evolving into wings.

*Tyrannosaurus
rex*

Forearm

Fused finger
bones

T rex's *sharp claws are
estimated to have been
6 in (15 cm) long*

T rex's *arms could have
been used to hold prey
at close quarters*

Puny props

For its great size, *Tyrannosaurus* had astonishingly tiny arms and hands. They were about as long as those of an adult human, but the bones were much thicker, and were heavily muscled. Injuries like ripped tendons are known and suggest the arms had some sort of use, perhaps when controlling prey or during mating.

Claws and their uses

Claws can tell us much about how dinosaurs lived. Predatory dinosaurs used sharp, curved claws as weapons. Several maniraptoran groups, such as the dromaeosaurids, had large foot claws used to puncture prey. But the longest claws of all belonged to the strange plant-eating theropod, *Therizinosaurus*. Herbivores that walked on all fours had short and simple hand claws because they were used only to support weight. Some ornithischians may have used their claws for digging up plants or burrowing.

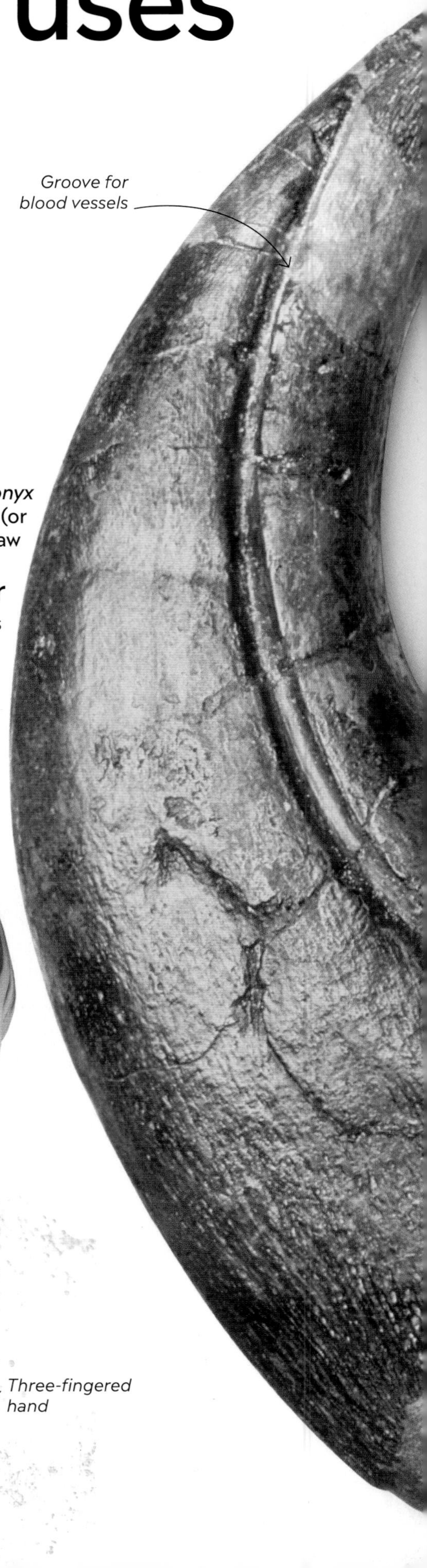

Groove for blood vessels

Baryonyx thumb (or finger) claw

Baryonyx ("heavy claw") got its name from the large, curved **claw** on its thumb or index finger.

A fishy hunter

Baryonyx patrolled the lake edges and floodplains of Europe in search of prey. Its skull with long jaws could plunge into water easily, helping it catch a variety of prey, including fish. It's been suggested *Baryonyx*'s enormous hand claw helped to scoop fish out of the water.

Baryonyx

Large claw

Three-fingered hand

Sharp tip

Super scythes

Therizinosaurus's fingers ended in enormous scythe-like claws. A horny sheath covered each claw and at least one claw was longer than a man's arm. *Therizinosaurus* most likely used its claws to rake leafy branches to its mouth.

Long finger claw

Gentle curve

Groove for horny sheath

Diplodocus foot bones

Digging tools

The flattened foot claws of sauropods may have been used to help dig out their nests. The overlapping nature of these claws may have formed a sort of spade to help carve out simple holes in the ground for their eggs, similar to some modern tortoises.

Little hooves

Triceratops's limbs bore little hooves shaped like a horse's. Three of the five fingers of each forelimb and all the toes ended in a broad, flat hoof bone with a horny covering. Hooves protected toes from wear, and the weight-bearing hoof bones helped support this horned dinosaur's heavy body as it walked.

Triceratops hoof bone

Triceratops

Deinonychus skeleton

To scale

Claws in action

Deinonychus ("terrible claw"), like other dromaeosaurids, had a large sickle claw on its raised second toe. These predators attacked prey that was smaller than them, using this claw for grip when they pinned a victim to the ground. Its feathered arms and rodlike tail helped it balance as the soon-to-be meal struggled.

Clawed finger

Tibia (shin bone)

Third toe

Fourth toe

Big, sharp, swiveling claw on second toe

Flock of ornithomimids

Long legs

Legs **and feet**

Fast-moving dinosaurs, such as theropods, walked and ran only on their hind limbs. The quickest dinosaurs had slim legs with long shins and narrow feet. In contrast, the heavy, plodding sauropods had thick, weight-bearing legs and short, broad feet. All dinosaurs walked on their toes and had vertical legs. The thigh bones fitted into the side of the hip bones through a ball-and-socket joint, similar to those in our hips.

👁 EYEWITNESS

On its toe
Paleontologist Neurides de Oliveira Martins discovered the fossil of a new desert-dwelling dinosaur in Brazil in 2019. Named *Vespersaurus*, this theropod had unusual feet. Its fossilized foot had three toes, but it rested its weight on the middle toe.

Tyrannosaurus

On the run
Tyrannosaurus was sometimes thought as a speedster, combining massive muscle power and agility to chase down prey. Yet, while it could turn more quickly than other big theropods, it could barely walk fast. Recent studies have shown that this heavy predator's leg bones would shatter if it ran. It is now thought to be a greater long-distance walker.

Heavy legs

The great escape

Ornithomimus ("bird mimic") was a long-legged dinosaur that resembled an ostrich, except for its arms and tail. Speed was its only defense and, like ostriches, ornithomimids could run fast. The metatarsals were wedged together to stabilize the foot, helping improve movement.

A flock of ornithomimids could sprint from danger at up to 40 mph (64 kph).

Theropod's foot

Theropods ("beast feet") get their name from their sharp, curved claws. A typical theropod foot, like this *Tyrannosaurus* foot, had three main toes, and a little hallux (big toe) that had evolved into a spike at the side of the foot.

Tibia

Long metatarsal

High ankle joint

Phalanx

Hallux

Plodding giant

Large sauropods, such as *Vulcanodon*, trudged along very slowly. Their leg bones had evolved not for running, but to support a huge, heavy body. Most sauropods were large enough to ignore most theropod predators.

Pillar-like limb

Vulcanodon

Sauropod's foot

Diplodocus's hind limbs were thick and strong to carry its weight. Each of the legs rested on a broad, three-clawed foot. The legs and feet of a sauropod resembled those of a modern elephant.

Massive tibia

Low ankle joint

Short metatarsal

Phalanx

BUILT FOR SPEED

Hypsilophodon's long leg bones—made up of the shin, calf, foot, and toe bones—show that this timid plant-eater could run fast. If it lived today, *Hypsilophodon* would stand no more than waist-high to a man, yet this small ornithopod could probably outrun an athlete.

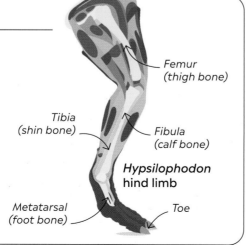

Femur (thigh bone)

Tibia (shin bone)

Fibula (calf bone)

Hypsilophodon hind limb

Metatarsal (foot bone)

Toe

Ancient footprints

Dinosaurs sometimes left their footprints in soft mud, which quickly dried and hardened. The footprints became buried in layers of mud, which turned into rock, preserving the footprints as fossils. The shapes and sizes of such prints and the gaps between them can help scientists identify which dinosaurs made the prints. They can also determine the rough sizes of the dinosaurs and how fast they moved.

👁 EYEWITNESS

Thunder foot

Fossil sauropod footprints found in rocks in Purgatoire in Colorado tell us that a herd of diplodocid dinosaurs passed by some time late in the Jurassic Period. Scientists were not sure exactly which dinosaur made the gigantic Purgatoire prints, so they gave it a special name—*Brontopodus*, meaning "thunder foot."

Ilium (hip bone)

Mantellisaurus skeleton

Hip height

Length of foot

Calculating size

Scientists can estimate the size of a dinosaur, such as this *Mantellisaurus*, from just its footprints without even seeing its fossil bones. Multiplying the size of a footprint by four gives an idea of the dinosaur's hip height. Scientists can then roughly work out the likely length of the whole animal.

Where hunters ran

This "dance floor" of dinosaur trackways appears to show a bustling ecosystem, but piecing together who made them, and whether they all interacted, is a difficult task for paleontologists.

Fossilized footprints are also known as ichnites

Numerous sets of dinosaur footprints could be evidence of
mass migration.

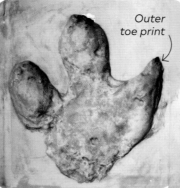

Outer toe print

Clover leaf clue

Fossil footprints shaped like a clover leaf often crop up in early Cretaceous rocks and belong to the blunt-toed ornithopod. At 11½ in (29 cm) long, this print was made by a young ornithopod weighing roughly 1,100 lb (500 kg). Theropods also make three-toed footprints, but these are usually narrower with more pointy toes.

Ornithopod's footprint

FOSSIL TRACKS

Scientists have identified 150,000 fossil tracks in a square patch of land 0.6 miles (1 km) across in Wyoming. Tracing individual dinosaur footprints can be difficult. As shown here, the survival of only the hind feet prints of a four-legged dinosaur might wrongly suggest that they came from a two-legged dinosaur.

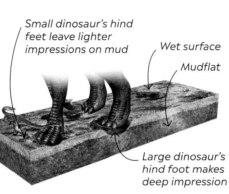

Small dinosaur's hind feet leave lighter impressions on mud

Wet surface

Mudflat

Large dinosaur's hind foot makes deep impression

Flood waters swirl in

Top layer of mud swirled away by current

Firmer layer of mud left intact

1. Making footprints
A small two-legged dinosaur and a large four-legged dinosaur both leave footprints on the surface mud, but only the large dinosaur's hind feet make dents in the firm lower layer.

2. Losing footprints
Water floods over the mudflat and washes away all the footprints made in the soft surface mud. Only the underprints formed in the lower layer survive.

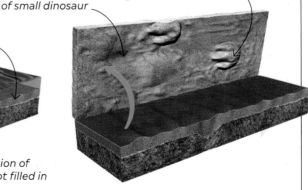

No impressions of small dinosaur

Convex impression of large dinosaur's hind foot

Flood waters retreating

Fresh mud deposited

Impression of hind foot filled in

3. Footprints fossilized
When the flood retreats, it leaves a layer of mud over the underprints. Over time, more floods dump mud in layers that harden into rock. Inside, the underprints survive as fossils.

4. Fossil prints revealed
Erosion causes the rock to wear away, revealing the fossil prints. As only hind feet prints survive, it is easy to assume that a two-legged dinosaur had made them.

Tough skins

A typical dinosaur's skin was waterproof and scaly, similar to that of a lizard or crocodile. The skin was also tough, so it was not easily cut in a fall or fight. The skin formed the first barrier against the environment and diseases, and also prevented precious water from being lost due to evaporation. Some dinosaur skin was reinforced with bony osteoderms and ossicles for extra protection.

Saltasaurus skin impression

Pea-size ossicles (bony lumps)

Saltasaurus

Armored hide

Countershading helped animals stay hidden

Psittacosaurus fossil

Tail quills

The preserved melanin in a Psittacosaurus can be seen without a microscope

Coat of armor

Some titanosaur sauropods, like the late Cretaceous *Saltasaurus*, had osteoderms embedded in the skin. Some osteoderms were the size of dinner plates, while others were pea-size ossicles. However, titanosaur armor was generally sparse.

Armored *Polacanthus* skin

Knobbly defense

This skin impression shows the knobbly plates that protected the ankylosaur *Polacanthus*. Spiky osteoderms on its neck, back, and tail guarded against the teeth and claws of hungry theropods. *Polacanthus* roamed western Europe around 130 million years ago.

Large, spiky osteoderm

Bony back

Many ankylosaurs had osteoderms on their backs. The osteoderm's flat underside was affixed to the animal's skin. The tiny pits on the upper surface show the positions of blood vessels. The plate was covered by a horny sheath made of keratin—the same material as our fingernails.

Ridge reinforced the bony plate

Bright pattern on skin

Reptilian skin

The Gila monster's skin is covered in bumpy scales arranged like tiny pebbles. From skin impressions preserved in rocks, we know that many dinosaurs had similar scales.

Fabulous fossil

Scientists discovered that some fossils preserve "melanosomes"—small structures that carry melanin pigments. These are found in the skin of many animals, including *Psittacosaurus*. Studying the melanosomes in the *Psittacosaurus* revealed that it was countershaded—lighter on the bottom and darker on top, camouflaging it from predators.

Patch of scaly skin

Scaly skin

A fossilized cast of a patch of skin from the hadrosaur *Edmontosaurus* shows a mass of little scales, which made the skin flexible. In places, there were also large, raised, conical scales. Some hadrosaurs had a fleshy crest on the head, like a small cockerel's comb.

Mud filled every tiny crease in the skin, creating this cast

Armored armadillo

Some modern mammals, such as armadillos, have similar defenses to those of the ankylosaurs. Bands of scutes (plates) run across an armadillo's body, and stiff shields guard the hips and shoulders. The weakest spot is the unprotected belly.

Feathers

Not all dinosaurs had scaly skin—some were covered in feathers. Discovered in Germany in 1861, *Archaeopteryx* was a primitive bird with wings, clawed fingers, and a long, bony tail. In 1996, scientists discovered *Sinosauropteryx*, a small, birdlike dinosaur with a downy covering on its body. The first feather-like structures might have been used for keeping the body warm. Feathers used for display and flight probably developed later.

Straight, feathered tail

Feathered tail

Feathered arm

Feathered or not?

In 2007, scientists found small bumps on a fossilized arm bone of the maniraptoran *Velociraptor*. Maniraptorans are the theropod group from which birds evolved. In birds, these bumps anchor feathers to the bone. With feathers found on its close fossil cousins, it is very probable that *Velociraptor* was feathered as well.

Batlike wings

Other ways to fly

Dinosaurs appear to have evolved flight more than once. The weird dinosaur *Yi qi* didn't have feathered wings like many of its cousins, but took to the air with batlike wing membranes. However, this experiment in flight ended here.

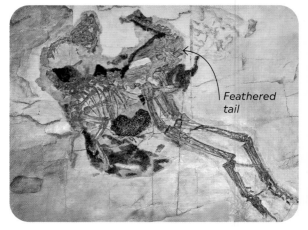

Feathered tail

Bright feathers

Caudipteryx had a short tail and feathers like a bird, yet its teeth and bones resembled those of other theropods. This theropod could not fly, but males probably showed off their bright feathers to attract a mate.

Taking to the sky

Modern birds are technically dinosaurs. The late Jurassic *Archaeopteryx* is considered to be the "first bird," but it had several dinosaurian features—teeth; clawed hands; and a long, bony tail. Its feathers helped generate some sort of powered flight as it flapped over what is now Germany.

Archaeopteryx

Small, light breastbone suggests muscles used in flight were small

Wing with long flight feathers

Feathered head

Feathered arm

Fossilized feathers

Fuzzy feathers

Scientists in China discovered *Sinornithosaurus*—a feathered dromaeosaurid. Traces of primitive fuzzy feathers line its bones. Its downy covering probably trapped body heat to keep it warm. Some scientists suggested it was venomous based on the shape of its teeth, but this idea was later overturned.

Outer wing feathers were as long as modern birds

Highly curved foot claw

Long tail feather

A bird with a beak

Like modern birds, *Confuciusornis* had a horny beak and fused tail bones. This helped it fly better than *Archaeopteryx*, yet it still had some primitive features such as clawed wing fingers. It lived in early Cretaceous China.

Feather shaft

Leading edge

Flight feathers

Archaeopteryx had asymmetrical feathers and wing bone shapes like those of modern flying birds. However, it appears to have flown in a unique style unseen in the modern world, probably taking to the air only in short bursts.

Eggs and young

Dinosaurs hatched from eggs, like birds and crocodiles. By studying a fossil eggshell, paleontologists can tell which type of dinosaur laid the egg, and reconstruct the body temperature of the mother using the eggshells. Sometimes a tiny skeleton can be found inside the fossil egg. Small dinosaurs probably sat on their eggs to warm them, but big dinosaurs hatched their eggs with the sun's warmth or rotting vegetation. Some hatchlings needed protection from predators, while others could find food on their own.

Hand

Stolen goods?

Oviraptor, and its relatives the oviraptorids, laid narrow, hard-shelled eggs. *Oviraptor* means "egg thief." Scientists once thought that *Oviraptor* stole eggs laid by plant-eater *Protoceratops*. They realized their mistake when they found fossils of an oviraptorid sitting on similar eggs to these.

Damage caused during fossilization

Oviraptor's fossilized egg

Head tucked in

Ready to hatch

This theropod embryo is nearly fully formed and it will soon begin exploring the outside world. Studies on rare dinosaur embryos have shown that they took between 3–6 months to hatch, which is more similar to reptiles than modern birds (11–85 days).

Foot

Warm bodies

By analyzing the different amounts of certain chemical elements locked away in fossil eggshells, it is possible to reconstruct the body temperatures of the mother that laid them. Some, like *Maiasaura*, may have been warmer than a person!

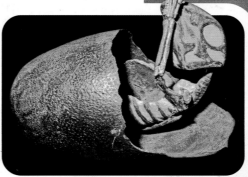

Neck

👁 EYEWITNESS

Soft shells
Paleontologists once believed that dinosaurs laid hard-shelled eggs, like crocodilians. However, in 2020 it was shown that ancestral dinosaurs likely laid soft-shelled eggs, like lizards. Some later dinosaur groups retained this egg type, while others evolved hard shells.

Growing up

From left to right, *Protoceratops* fossils show how this plant-eater's skull changed as it grew up. The beak became tall and narrow, the bony frill at the back of the skull grew bigger, and the cheeks flared out at the sides.

Hatchling

Egg

Beak becomes longer

Juvenile

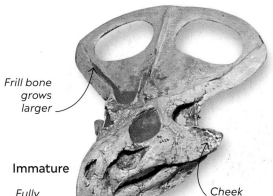

Frill bone grows larger

Immature

Fully grown frill

Cheek becomes wider

Fossilized *Citipati* with eggs

'Til death do us part

A sandstorm or collapsing dune overwhelmed oviraptorid *Citipati* while it incubated eggs in its nest. This particular *Citipati* died with its feathered arms spread out to shield the eggs from the weather. *Citipati* lived in what is now Mongolia's Gobi Desert.

Strong beak

Adult

59

Finding fossils

Fossil hunters looking for dinosaur bones must first identify the right kinds of rocks. Dinosaur fossils are usually found buried in sedimentary rocks like sandstones, in barren deserts, cliffs, and quarries. Discovering the bones is just the start. Field teams may work for weeks to excavate a large fossil without damaging it. Meanwhile, they measure, map, and photograph each bone.

Ancient treasure trove
In 1938, paleontologist Yang Zhongjian unearthed fossils of the prosauropod *Lufengosaurus* in China's Lufeng Basin. Since then, the area has yielded more than 100 dinosaur skeletons from the Jurassic Period. This paleontologist is excavating a sauropodomorph skeleton in the region.

Quarry maps
Grid lines are placed in the field so the position of the bones can be mapped. This is important, as it tells of the processes that occurred during burial.

Gloves

Straight-headed hammer for splitting hard rock

Pointed chisel

Flat chisel

Curved-headed brick hammer for breaking up and clearing softer rocks, such as clays

Rock saw for cutting through rock

The find

When excavating dinosaur bones, paleontologists use hammers and chisels to clear away the rocky material surrounding the bones. Next, they wrap the bones in sackcloth soaked in wet plaster. This sets quickly, forming a strong, rigid coat. Each plaster jacket protects the fragile fossil bone inside against damage on the ride to the laboratory.

1 Cleaning a limb bone
The paleontologists carefully brush away dirt from the fossil bone before encasing it in plaster.

2 Making a plaster cast
Then they apply runny plaster of Paris to sackcloth bandages and wrap these around the bone.

3 Preparing for study
When the bone arrives at the laboratory, technicians remove the cast so the bone can be studied.

Tools of the trade

Paleontologists use tools like these to free fossils from rock, to clean them, and to pack them safely. They might paint fragile bones with watery glue to stop them from crumbling, and then encase the bones in a plaster jacket. Or they might wrap the bones in aluminum foil and then pour on chemicals producing polyurethane foam, which expands and covers the fossils to protect them.

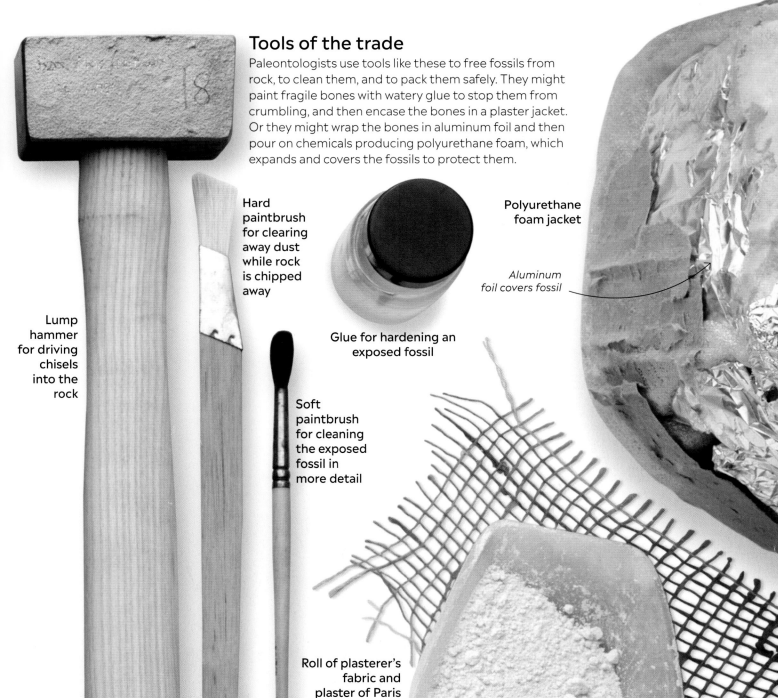

Hard paintbrush for clearing away dust while rock is chipped away

Polyurethane foam jacket

Aluminum foil covers fossil

Glue for hardening an exposed fossil

Lump hammer for driving chisels into the rock

Soft paintbrush for cleaning the exposed fossil in more detail

Roll of plasterer's fabric and plaster of Paris

Rebuilding a dinosaur

Digging up a dinosaur's bones is the first step in learning what it looked like. Museum technicians saw off the plaster coats protecting the bones and chip away any hard rock with chisels. They use tools like dentists' drills for detailed work, and may even use acid on certain kinds of stone. Using the clean bones, paleontologists can reconstruct the dinosaur's skeleton by fitting them together. Model-makers can then build a lifelike restoration of the animal.

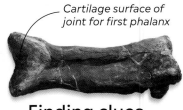

Cartilage surface of joint for first phalanx

Finding clues

Fossil bones can tell us about muscles and other tissues that have vanished. The upper end of this *Iguanodon* foot bone shows where cartilage (gristle) protected the ankle joint. The bottom end is where cartilage protected the bone against the first toe bone (phalanx).

Exposing the fossil

A technician uses acid to reveal embryos hidden in fossil dinosaur eggs. Each day, acid eats away a wafer-thin layer of the stony material around the embryos. This process can take up to a year.

On display

This reconstructed skeleton of a *Tyrannosaurus rex* is displayed at the Field Museum in Illinois. Museums worldwide display replicas, which are cast from molds made from real fossils.

T rex *skeleton reconstructed from fossils*

Scanning dinosaurs

In order to reconstruct dinosaurs, professionals can use a range of scanning techniques to piece the bones back together. Handheld scanners produce 3D images of the surface of dinosaur bones, which can then be moved and connected to other bones to complete the skeleton.

Baryonyx restoration

Model

A sculptor made this realistic model of a freshly dead *Baryonyx* by studying the way the dinosaur's bones were arranged on the flood plain when paleontologists dug them up. Scientists then worked out where to add the muscles, skin, and other tissues.

Reconstruction of flood plain

T rex skeleton at the Field Museum in Chicago

Dinosaurs inside out

Another type of scanning technique uses powerful CT scanners to see inside the bones. This allows scientists to understand the anatomy of internal structures without breaking apart the precious fossil. Here, the braincase of the predator *Arcovenator* is being scanned.

The complete picture

To understand a dinosaur specimen better, it helps to look at evidence beyond the bare bones. Soil and microfossils discovered at a dig site are examined in the lab. It places a dinosaur in the context of its ecosystem, allowing paleontologists to reconstruct the ecosystem it inhabited.

Classifying dinosaurs

Members of a species have a unique set of characteristics that differentiate them from those of another species. The differences and similarities between species help build family trees. Shared traits, inherited from a common ancestor, create a "clade." The main dinosaur clades are shown here.

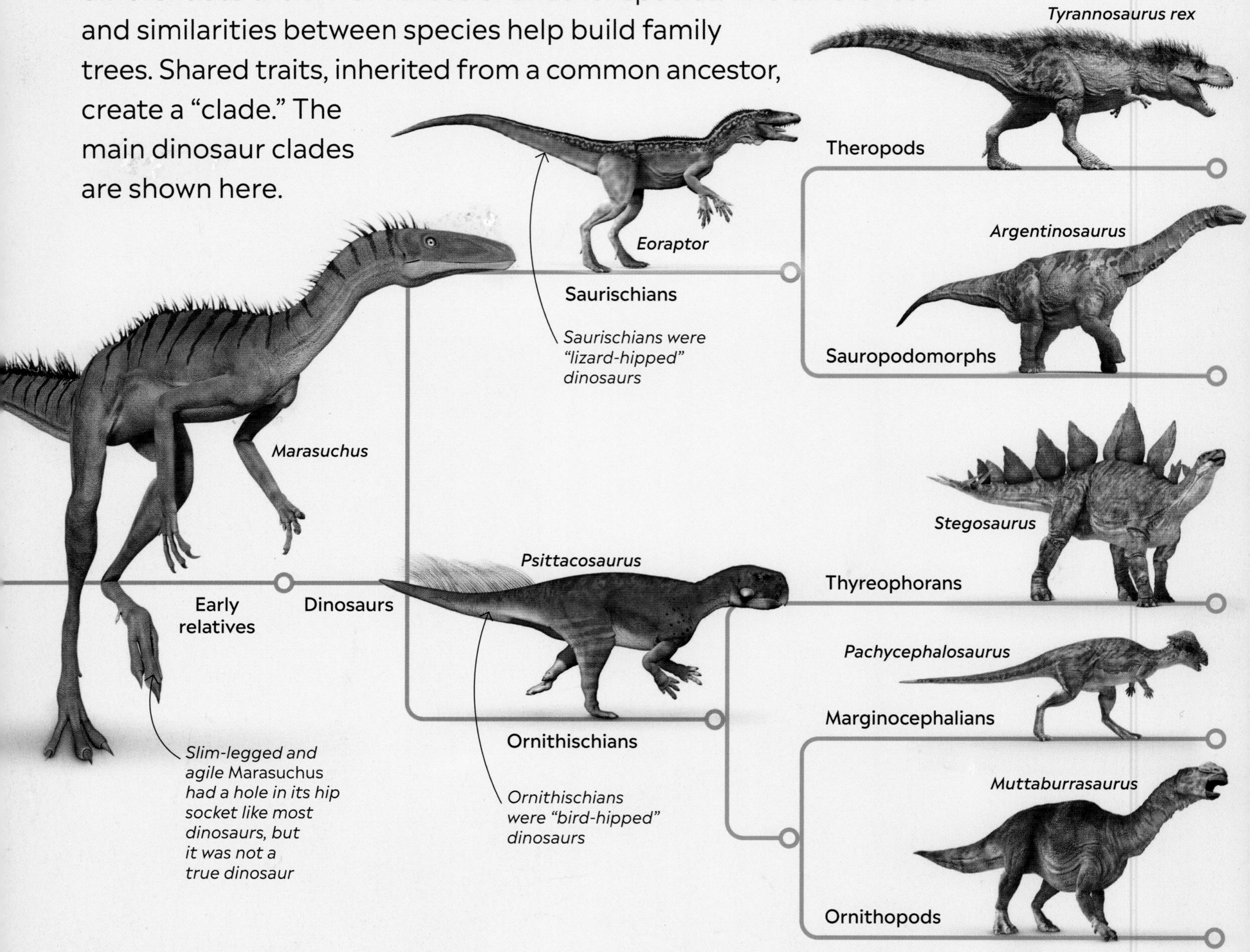

Tyrannosaurus rex

Theropods

Eoraptor

Argentinosaurus

Saurischians

Saurischians were "lizard-hipped" dinosaurs

Sauropodomorphs

Marasuchus

Stegosaurus

Psittacosaurus

Thyreophorans

Early relatives

Dinosaurs

Pachycephalosaurus

Marginocephalians

Ornithischians

Ornithischians were "bird-hipped" dinosaurs

Slim-legged and agile Marasuchus had a hole in its hip socket like most dinosaurs, but it was not a true dinosaur

Muttaburrasaurus

Ornithopods

NEW FAMILY TREE

In 2017, a new dinosaur family tree was proposed. By looking closely at some of the oldest dinosaurs, paleontologist Matthew Baron and his team suggested that theropods and ornithischians are actually closely related. Herrerasaurids, usually thought of as theropods, may even be cousins to sauropodomorphs. Time will tell if this new tree is correct.

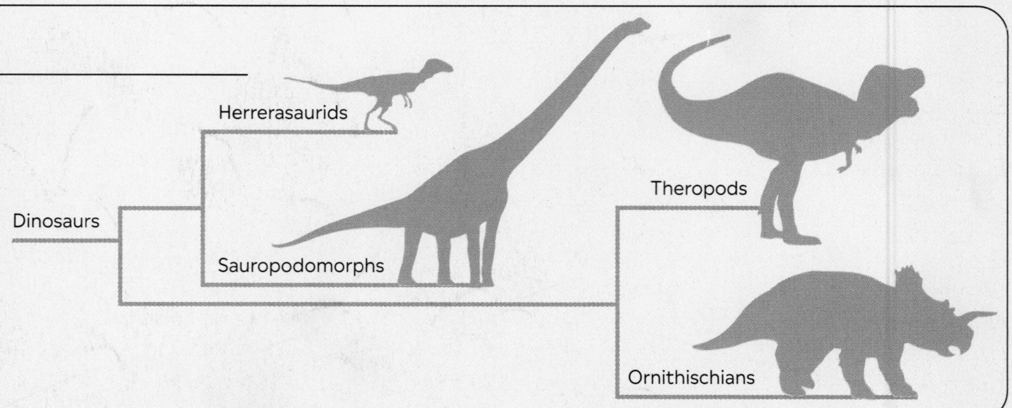

Herrerasaurids

Dinosaurs

Sauropodomorphs

Theropods

Ornithischians

Pronunciation guide

Naming dinosaurs

Most dinosaurs' scientific names are based on Latin or Greek words and each name means something. For instance, *Triceratops* ("three-horned face") describes a special anatomical feature. Many names are tricky to say, but our guide below helps you pronounce many of those in the book.

Huayangosaurus

Name	Pronunciation	Name	Pronunciation
Albertosaurus	al-BERT-oh-SORE-us	*Iguanodon*	ig-GWAH-no-don
Allosaurus	AL-oh-SORE-us	*Kentrosaurus*	KEN-troh-SORE-us
Alxasaurus	ALK-sah-SORE-us	*Lambeosaurus*	LAMB-ee-oh-SORE-us
Amargasaurus	ah-MAR-gah-SORE-us	*Leaellynasaura*	lee-ELL-in-ah-SORE-ah
Anchisaurus	ankee-SORE-us	*Lesothosaurus*	li-SUE-too-SORE-us
Ankylosaurus	ANK-ill-oh-SORE-us	*Maiasaura*	MY-a-SORE-a
Apatosaurus .	a-PAT-oh-SORE-us	*Majungatholus*	mah-JOONG-gah-THOL-uss
Archaeopteryx	ar-kee-OP-ter-ix	*Mamenchisaurus*	ma-MEN-chee-SORE-us
Argentinosaurus	ARE-jen-TEEN-oh-SORE-us	*Megalosaurus*	MEG-ah-low-SORE-us
Bambiraptor	BAM-bee-RAP-tor	*Mei long*	may-LOONG
Barapasaurus	buh-RAH-pah-SORE-us	*Microraptor*	MY-crow-RAP-tor
Barosaurus	BAH-roe-SORE-us	*Monolophosaurus*	MON-oh-LOAF-oh-SORE-us
Barsboldia	bahrs-BOHL-dee-uh	*Muttaburrasaurus*	MOO-tah-BUH-ruh-SORE-us
Baryonyx	bah-ree-ON-ix	*Nigersaurus*	nee-ZHAYR-SORE-us
Brachiosaurus	brackee-oh-SORE-us	*Ornithomimus*	OR-nith-oh-MIME-us
Camarasaurus	KAM-a-ra-SORE-us	*Ouranosaurus*	oo-RAH-noh-SORE-us
Camptosaurus	CAMP-toe-SORE-us	*Oviraptor*	OH-vee-RAP-tor
Carcharodontosaurus	CAR-ka-roe-DON-toe-SORE-us	*Pachycephalosaurus*	PACK-ee-SEF-ah-low-SORE-us
Carnotaurus	car-noe-TORE-us	*Pachyrhinosaurus*	PACK-ee-RINE-oh-SORE-us
Caudipteryx	caw-DIP-ter-ix	*Parasaurolophus*	PA-ra-SORE-oh-LOAF-us
Centrosaurus	cen-TROH-SORE-us	*Pentaceratops*	PEN-ta-SERRA-tops
Ceratosaurus	ser-AT-oh-SORE-us	*Plateosaurus*	PLATE-ee-oh-SORE-us
Citipati	SIH-tee-PAH-tee	*Polacanthus*	pol-a-KAN-thuss
Coelophysis	SEE-low-FYE-sis	*Protoceratops*	PRO-toe-SERRA-tops
Compsognathus	COMP-sog-NAITH-us	*Psittacosaurus*	SIT-ack-oh-SORE-us
Confuciusornis	con-FEW-shus-OR-niss	*Saltasaurus*	SALT-ah-SORE-us
Corythosaurus	ko-RITH-oh-SORE-us	*Sauropelta*	SORE-oh-PELT-ah
Cryolophosaurus	CRY-uh-LOF-uh-SORE-us	*Scelidosaurus*	SKELL-ih-doe-SORE-us
Deinocheirus	DINE-oh-KIRE-us	*Sinornithosaurus*	sine-OR-nith-oh-SORE-us
Deinonychus	dye-NON-ee-cus	*Sinosauropteryx*	SIGH-no-sore-OP-ter-ix
Dilophosaurus	die-LOAF-oh-SORE-us	*Sinraptor*	SIN-rap-tor
Diplodocus	dip-LOD-oh-kus	*Spinosaurus*	SPINE-oh-SORE-us
Dryosaurus	DRY-oh-SORE-us	*Stegoceras*	STEG-o-SER-ass
Edmontonia	ED-mon-TOE-nee-a	*Stegosaurus*	STEG-oh-SORE-us
Edmontosaurus	ed-MONT-oh-SORE-us	*Styracosaurus*	sty-RACK-oh-SORE-us
Eocursor	EE-oh-KER-sor	*Tarbosaurus*	TAR-bow-SORE-us
Eoraptor	EE-oh-rap-tor	*Tenontosaurus*	ten-NON-toe-SORE-us
Epidexipteryx	epi-dex-IP-terricks	*Therizinosaurus*	THERRY-zin-oh-SORE-us
Euoplocephalus	YOU-owe-plo-SEFF-ah-lus	*Tianyulong confucius*	Tee-AN-ee-OO-long CON-fe-YOO-shus
Gallimimus	GAL-ih-MIME-us	*Triceratops*	try-SERRA-tops
Gastonia	gas-TOE-nee-a	*Troodon*	TROH-oh-don
Giganotosaurus	jig-AN-oh-toe-SORE-us	*Tyrannosaurus*	TIE-ran-oh-SORE-us
Guanlong	GWON-long	*Velociraptor*	vel-OSS-ee-RAP-tor
Herrerasaurus	her-air-ah-SORE-us	*Vespersaurus*	VESS-perr-SORE-us
Heterodontosaurus	HET-er-oh-DON-toe-SORE- us	*Vulcanodon*	vul-KAN-o-don
Huayangosaurus	HWAH-YANG-oh-SORE-us	*Yi qi*	Yee-key
Hypsilophodon	HIP-sih-LOAF-oh-don		

Discovery timeline

Since the first discovery of dinosaur bones in the 1600s, fossil hunters have unearthed and named more than 600 different dinosaurs. Fossils help scientists work out how dinosaurs moved, fed, fought, bred, and died. This timeline highlights the milestones in the study of dinosaurs.

1677
English curator Robert Plot illustrates part of a *Megalosaurus* thigh bone in a book. He believes it to be the bone of a giant man.

1818
Fossil bones found in Connecticut will later prove to be the first discovery of a North American dinosaur—*Anchisaurus*.

1820
Gideon Mantell, a British doctor, begins to collect fossils of a giant reptile that he later names and describes as *Iguanodon*.

1824
Megalosaurus is the first dinosaur to receive an official scientific name when Britain's William Buckland describes its fossil jaw.

1842
The name "Dinosauria" appears in print for the first time after British anatomist Sir Richard Owen realizes that three kinds of giant fossil reptiles formed part of a special group.

1859
Dinosaur eggshells are first discovered in the south of France.

1861
German paleontologist Hermann von Meyer describes *Archaeopteryx*, a bird with feathered wings, but with the teeth and bony tail of a dinosaur.

1878
Belgian coalminers find fossils of dozens of *Iguanodon* at a depth of 1,056 ft (322 m).

1888
British paleontologist Harry Govier Seeley splits dinosaurs into two main groups—the Saurischia (lizard-hipped) and the Ornithischia (bird-hipped).

1902
American fossil hunter Barnum Brown finds the first *Tyrannosaurus* skeleton in Montana.

1915
German paleontologist Ernst Stromer von Reichenbach names *Spinosaurus*.

1922–1925
In Mongolia, Roy Chapman Andrews, Henry Fairfield Osborn, and Walter Granger find fossils of dinosaurs including *Oviraptor*, *Protoceratops*, and *Velociraptor*.

1925
In Algeria, French paleontologists Charles Depéret and J. Savornin discover the teeth of *Carcharodontosaurus*.

1933–1970s
Chinese paleontologist Yang Zhongjian names *Lufengosaurus*, *Mamenchisaurus*, *Tsintaosaurus*, and *Omeisaurus*.

1941
American paleontologist Roland T Bird describes sauropod footprints, showing that some dinosaurs traveled in herds.

1954
Russian paleontologist Evgeny Maleev discovers the long claws of *Therizinosaurus*, but thinks they belong to a giant turtle.

1963–1971
Two Polish-Mongolian expeditions to the Gobi Desert unearth the remains of a *Velociraptor* locked in battle with a *Protoceratops*. One of the members of these expeditions, Halszka Osmólska, names many new groups.

1969
American paleontologist John Ostrom argues that dinosaurs were active and warm-blooded. He also claims that birds evolved from small theropods. His ideas change the way scientists viewed dinosaurs.

1972
American paleontologist Robert Bakker suggests that air sacs in some dinosaurs reveal that these must have had a breathing system like that of birds. Later research supports this idea, at least for saurischian (lizard-hipped) dinosaurs.

1974
Paleontologists Peter Galton and Robert Bakker publish a paper where they argue that birds are actually dinosaurs. Subsequent research provides support for their claim.

1978
American paleontologists John Horner and Robert Makela find the first evidence that dinosaurs cared for their young.

1980
American geologist Walter Alvarez and his nuclear physicist father Luis Alvarez establish that a large asteroid smashed into Earth at the end of the Cretaceous Period with devastating effects.

1984
British paleontologist Michael Benton coins the name "Dinosauromorpha" for the group of reptiles consisting of dinosaurs and their closest relatives.

1986
British paleontologists Alan Charig and Angela Milner describe a fish-eating theropod *Baryonyx*, identified as a relative of *Spinosaurus*.

1991
American paleontologist William Hammer excavates *Cryolophosaurus*. In 1994, it becomes the first Antarctic dinosaur to be named.

1993
Argentinian paleontologists José Bonaparte and Jaimé Powell describe the immense sauropod *Argentinosaurus*.

American paleontologist Paul Sereno describes *Eoraptor*, the earliest dinosaur to be discovered so far.

1995
Argentinian paleontologists Rodolfo Coria and Leonardo Salgado describe *Giganotosaurus*, a massive theropod.

1998
Chinese paleontologists Chen Pei-ji, Dong Zhi-ming, and Zhen Shuo-nan describe *Sinosauropteryx*, the first known dinosaur with skin covered in down rather than in reptilian scales.

Carcharodontosaurus skull compared with human skull

Karen Chin examining coprolites

1998
American paleontologist Karen Chin describes tyrannosaur coprolites (fossil dung) that contains bones from a horned dinosaur.

2003
Six Chinese paleontologists describe *Microraptor gui*, a small theropod with feathered arms and legs.

American paleontologists Raymond Rogers, David Krause, and Kristina Curry Rogers show that theropod *Majungasaurus* ate others of its kind, proving that some dinosaurs were cannibals.

2005
Several paleontologists including Meng Jin and Wang Yuanqing find fossils from early Cretaceous China showing that some mammals ate baby dinosaurs.

Swedish scientist Caroline Strömberg and her colleagues show that some sauropods ate grass in India. Until this discovery, people thought that grass did not exist in the Age of Dinosaurs.

2007
American and Japanese paleontologists find evidence that some dinosaurs lived in burrows. In an underground den, they found fossils of the ornithopod *Oryctodromeus*.

2009
Paleontologist Mary Schweitzer and colleagues in the US describe the oldest known protein from an 80-million-year-old hadrosaur's thigh bone. Protein analysis indicates that ornithischian dinosaurs were more closely related to living birds than to alligators.

Tianyulong, a tiny ornithischian with long quills, is discovered. It may be related to bird feathers, pushing back the origin of feathers to the first dinosaur, and maybe beyond.

2010
Two different teams publish on the fossilized colors of two feathered dinosaurs: *Sinosauropteryx* and *Anchiornis*. The former was a rusty orange with a striped tail, while the other was black and white with a red crest.

2011
Dromaeosaurids are shown to have used their sickle claws not to slash prey open, but instead to grip and pin them down.

2012
Microraptor is shown to have black, iridescent feathers by Quango Li and other researchers, after they study fossilized pigments found in some of its feathers.

Dr. Xing Xu sitting among the remains of duck-billed dinosaurs in Zhucheng, China in 2012

Xing Xu and colleagues discover and name *Yutyrannus*, a large, feathered tyrannosaur.

2013
Scott Sampson and colleagues officially name *Nasutoceratops*, an unusual ceratopsian with bull-like features.

2014
New material of the enigmatic *Spinosaurus* is unearthed in Egypt by Nizar Ibrahim and colleagues. More of this specimen would then be discovered and published in 2019.

2015
Brontosaurus, which was thought to be a specimen of *Apatosaurus* for over 100 years, is shown to be a separate animal by Emanuel Tschopp and colleagues.

Dakotaraptor, a large dromaeosaurid from the late Cretaceous, is named and described by Robert DePalma and a team of researchers.

2016
A feathered tail of a small theropod is found preserved in Burmese amber.

Aaron LeBlanc directs research into the complex dental batteries of hadrosaurids, showing that their teeth developed in a way that is not similar to that in any modern animal.

2017
Sara Burch explores the muscle groups in the unusually small forelimbs of *Majungasaurus*, showing they likely had some sort of function.

The discovery of an exquisitely preserved ankylosaur, called *Borealopelta*, provides new insight into its biology. Fossil pigments show it had a reddish back and pale belly, a type of camouflage suggesting it was under threat.

Matthew Barron and colleagues publish a new family tree of the dinosaurs, placing theropods closer to ornithischians than to sauropods. Time will tell if this new tree replaces the traditional split first suggested by Harry Govier Seeley in 1888.

2018
Hesham Sallam and coauthors describe the sauropod *Mansourasaurus* from Egypt, proving that African dinosaurs may have been related to Asian and European sauropods in the late Cretaceous.

Auguste Hassler and colleagues measure chemical signals from North African fossils to show that spinosaurs were eating more aquatic prey compared to other large theropods in the region, helping them coexist.

2019
Jingmai O'Connor leads research looking at the evolution of the digestive system in birds and their fossil relatives.

New methods help Michael Lee and his team determine that South America was the likely place where dinosaurs first evolved.

Victoria Arbour and Lindsay Zanno show that the tail clubs of ankylosaurs and glyptodonts from the Cenozoic evolved for similar uses despite being unrelated.

2020
Susannah Maidment leads a team of researchers to name *Adratiklit*, the oldest stegosaur and the first from North Africa.

Alessandro Chiarenza and colleagues show that the asteroid impact at Chicxulub, Mexico, and not volcanic eruptions, was responsible for the extinction of the non-bird dinosaurs.

Chemical analysis of dinosaur eggshells show that dinosaurs were warm-blooded, with some ornithopods such as *Maiasaura* having body temperatures around 104°F (40°C).

Find out more

There are many ways of finding out about dinosaurs apart from reading books. You can study dinosaur skeletons in museums or see exhibitions of lifelike dinosaur models. You can also take virtual museum tours on the Internet. Then there are dinosaur films and television documentaries that feature scarily realistic models and computer-generated images.

Hunting for dinosaur fossils

Good hunting grounds for fossils include rocks below cliffs that are made of clay, mudstone, and sandstone from the Mesozoic Era. Permission is needed to visit some sites, and hunters should keep away from cliffs where rocks could fall.

Museum skeletons

Fossil dinosaurs in museums are made of bones or copies of bones fitted together and supported by rods. The exhibits show how dinosaurs stood when they were alive. Touring exhibitions often include skeletons from distant parts of the world.

Kentrosaurus **skeleton at the Museum für Naturkunde, Berlin, Germany**

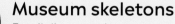

Rocks from the Jurassic Period containing dinosaur bones

Up close

Here, in Pittsburgh's Carnegie Museum of Natural History, children watch paleontologist Alan Tabrum tackle the huge and well-preserved skull of Samson, a *Tyrannosaurus rex*—a two-year task.

Join a dig!

You might be able to see experts working at a fossil site, or even join in. For years, people have watched paleontologists carefully ease out bones from rock at the Dinosaur National Monument in Utah.

Building dinosaurs

Children enjoy building dinosaurs in Boston Public Schools, which collaborated with the Children's Museum. The museum also hosts *Explore·a·Saurus*, an interactive exhibit where children can touch fossil footprints and work a life-size dinosaur model.

A 3D dinosaur puzzle for children

PLACES TO VISIT

- **Natural History Museum, Cromwell Road, London, UK**
Includes one of the most complete *Stegosaurus* skeletons ever found.
- **Dinosaur Isle Museum, Isle of Wight**
Home to iconic British dinosaurs such as *Neovenator*, fossil walks are organized and their specialists are on hand to help identify any dinosaur bones you find on the nearby beaches.
- **Museum Für Naturkunde Invalidenstrasse, Berlin, Germany**
Includes a *Giraffatitan*, the world's tallest mounted dinosaur skeleton.
- **Field Museum of Natural History, Lake Shore Drive, Chicago**
Has the world's largest *Tyrannosaurus*. Houses an enormous skeleton of the giant titanosaur *Patagotitan*.
- **Royal Tyrrell Museum Of Palaeontology Drumheller, Canada**
Displays 40 mounted fossil skeletons.
- **Beijing Museum Of Natural History Tianqiao South Street, Beijing, China**
Displays fossils of feathered dinosaurs.
- **Fukui Prefectural Dinosaur, Museumterao, Muroka, Katsuyama, Japan**
Has the largest dinosaur display in Japan with 45 skeletons.
- **Muséum National d'Histoire Naturelle, Paris, France**
An impressive bone collection, evolution gallery, and skeletons of *Allosaurus* and Carnotaurus can be found at this institution.
- **Museo Paleontologico Egidio Feruglio, Chubut, Argentina**
Includes giant skeletons of Argentina's past, such as *Tyrannotitan*.

Real on reel

A *Tyrannosaurus rex* threatens a man in this scene from *Jurassic World: Fallen Kingdom* (2018). With computer-generated dinosaur images and robotic models, the *Jurassic World* films make dinosaurs look lifelike, even though they might not have accurately represented the actual dinosaurs.

Glossary

Ammonites An extinct group of mollusks related to squid; with a coiled shell. They lived in Mesozoic seas.

Amphibians A group of cold-blooded vertebrates (backboned animals) that appeared more than 100 million years before the dinosaurs. The young live in fresh water but many grow into land-based adults. Living examples include frogs.

Ankylosaurs ("fused lizards") A group of four-legged, armored, plant-eating ornithischians with bony plates covering the neck, shoulders, and back, and a horny beak used for cropping plants.

Archosaurs A group of extinct and living reptiles with two main subgroups. Crocodiles and their relatives form one group. Dinosaurs, pterosaurs, and their relatives form the other.

Asteroid A rocky lump orbiting the sun. Asteroids are smaller than planets but can measure hundreds of miles across.

Bipedal Walking on two hind limbs, rather than on all fours.

Cycad

Bipedal (*Giganotosaurus*)

Birds A group of dinosaurs with feathered wings. Some scientists call the whole group Aves. Others call the modern birds Aves and refer to the extinct birds as Avialae.

Ceratopsians ("horned faces") Plant-eating ornithischians, with a deep beak and a bony frill at the back of the skull. Many, such as *Triceratops*, had facial horns.

Cold-blooded Animals that are cold-blooded are dependent upon the sun's heat for body warmth. Most reptiles are cold-blooded (*see also* Warm-blooded).

Conifer A cone-bearing tree such as a pine or fir.

Cretaceous Period Third period of the Mesozoic Era; about 145–66 million years ago.

Cycad A palm-shaped, seed-bearing plant with long, fernlike leaves. Cycads were common during the Age of Dinosaurs.

Dromaeosaurids ("running lizards") A group of birdlike theropods that were related to birds.

Duck-billed dinosaurs *See* Hadrosaurs

Embryo A plant, animal, or other organism in an early stage of development from an egg or a seed.

Evolution The gradual changes in living organisms that occur over many generations. Evolution may result in new species. Dinosaurs gradually evolved from reptile ancestors, and birds evolved, step by step, from dinosaurs.

Extinction The dying-out of a plant or animal species.

Fossil The remains of something that once lived, preserved in rock. Teeth and bones are more likely to form fossils than softer body parts, such as skin, muscles, or internal organs.

Genus (plural, genera) In the classification of living organisms, a group of closely related species. The species *Tyrannosaurus rex* belongs to the genus *Tyrannosaurus*.

Ginkgo A unique type of broadleaved tree with triangular leaves that evolved in the Triassic Period and survives to this day. A type of gymnosperm.

Gymnosperms One of the two main types of land plants that produce seeds. It includes cycads, ginkgoes, and conifers, such as pine and fir.

Hadrosaurs ("bulky lizards") Duck-billed dinosaurs. Large, bipedal and quadrupedal ornithopods from late in the Cretaceous Period. They had a ducklike beak that was used for browsing on vegetation.

Ichthyosaurs Large prehistoric reptiles with a pointed head, flippers, and a fishlike tail. *Ichthyosaurs* were streamlined for swimming fast in the sea. Most lived in the Jurassic Period.

Jurassic Period Second period of the Mesozoic Era; about 201–145 million years ago.

Mammals Warm-blooded vertebrates that feed their young on milk. Their skin is covered in hair or fur. Mammals began to appear in the Triassic Period.

Maniraptorans ("grasping hands") A group of theropods with long arms and hands, including dromaeosaurids, such as *Velociraptor*, and birds.

Mesozoic ("middle life") The geological era, about 252–66 million years ago, containing the Triassic, Jurassic, and Cretaceous periods. From the late Triassic on, dinosaurs were the dominant land animals in the Mesozoic.

Mammal (*Negabaata*)

Mollusks Snails, clams, squid, and their relatives. Ammonites belonged to a group of mollusks called cephalopods.

Mosasaurs Large, aquatic lizards with paddle-shaped limbs and a flattened tail. They hunted fish and other sea creatures in the Cretaceous Period.

Ornithischians ("bird hips") One of the two main dinosaur groups (see also Saurischians). In ornithischians, the pelvis (hip bone) is similar to that of birds. Ornithischians include stegosaurs, ceratopsians, pachycephalosaurs, ankylosaurs, and ornithopods.

Ornithopods ("bird feet") A group of plant-eating ornithischians with long hind limbs. The group includes *Iguanodon* and hadrosaurs.

Pachycephalosaurs ("thick-headed lizards") A group of bipedal ornithischians with a thick skull.

Paleontologist Scientist who studies the fossil remains of plants and animals.

Paleontology The scientific study of fossilized organisms.

Paleozoic ("ancient life") The geological era before the Mesozoic. It lasted from 540 until 252 million years ago.

Plesiosaurs A group of large marine reptiles living in the Mesozoic Era, often with flipper-shaped limbs and a long neck.

Predator An animal or plant that preys on animals for food.

Paleozoic Era
(Trilobite fossil)

Prosauropods ("before sauropods") A group of early plant-eating saurischians that lived from late in the Triassic Period to early in the Jurassic Period.

Psittacosaurs ("parrot lizards") Bipedal ceratopsians living in the Cretaceous Period. Psittacosaurs had deep beaks like those of parrots and used them to eat plants.

Pterosaurs ("winged lizards") Flying reptiles of the Mesozoic Era, related to the dinosaurs.

Quadrupedal Walking on all fours.

Radioactive element A substance that decays by giving off particles and energy. Scientists can find the age of fossil-bearing rocks by measuring the radioactivity of elements found in volcanic rocks just above or just below the fossil-bearing rocks.

Reptiles Typically, cold-blooded, scaly vertebrates that lay eggs or give birth on land. Living reptiles include lizards, snakes, turtles, and crocodiles.

Saurischians ("lizard hips") One of two main dinosaur groups (see also Ornithischians). In typical saurischians, the hip bones are similar to those of lizards. Saurischians include prosauropods, sauropods, and theropods.

Sauropods ("lizard feet") Huge, quadrupedal, plant-eating saurischians, with long necks and tails. They lived through most of the Mesozoic Era.

Scute A bony plate with a horny covering to protect the dinosaur from an enemy's teeth and claws.

Sediment Material, such as sand and mud, deposited by wind, water, or ice.

Skull The bony framework protecting the brain, eyes, ears, and nasal passages.

Species The level below genus in the classification of living things. Individuals in a species can breed to produce fertile young. Each species has a two-part name *Microraptor gui*, for instance.

Stegosaurs ("plated/roofed lizards") Plant-eating, quadrupedal ornithischians with two tall rows of bony plates running down the neck, back, and tail.

Theropods ("beast feet") Mostly predatory saurischians with sharp teeth and claws.

Trace fossil The remains of signs of prehistoric creatures, rather than fossils of the creatures themselves, preserved in rock. Trace fossils include footprints, bite marks, droppings, eggs, and fossil impressions of skin, hair, and feathers.

Fossil droppings

Triassic Period First period of the Mesozoic Era; about 252–201 million years ago.

Tyrannosaurids ("tyrant lizards") Huge, bipedal theropods with a large head, short arms, two-fingered hands, and massive hind limbs. Tyrannosaurids flourished late in the Cretaceous Period in North America and Asia.

Vertebrates Animals with a spinal column, or backbone.

Warm-blooded Keeping the body at constant temperature (often above that of the surroundings) by turning energy from food into heat. Many dinosaurs were probably warm-blooded, although modern reptiles are not. Mammals and birds are warm-blooded (see also Cold-blooded).

Sauropod
(*Mamenchisaurus*)

Index

AB

Acanthostega 24
Albertosaurus 15
Allosaurus, jaws and teeth 32–33
Amargasaurus 45
ammonites 17, 18–19
amniotes 24
Anchisaurus 12
ankylosaurs 12, 14, 21, 30, 55
Ankylosaurus 26, 43
Apatosaurus 42
Archaeopteryx 13, 57
archosaurs 11, 24
Argentinosaurus 22
armadillos 55
asteroid 16–17
Bajadasaurus 36–37
Bambiraptor 47
Barosaurus 23
Baryonyx 32, 48, 63
birds 12, 16, 56–57
  ancestors of 14
  evolution 46
  survivors 17
body temperatures 58
Brachiosaurus 22
brains 26–27, 29
Brown, Barnum 21
Buckland, William 20

CD

Camarasaurus 26, 47
Carcharodontosaurus 22
Carnotaurus 28, 41
Caudipteryx 56
ceratopsians 8
ceratopsids 36
chalk 17
Chicxulub crater 17
Chin, Karen 67
Citipati 33, 58–59
classifying dinosaurs 64–65
coccolithophores 17
Coelophysis 11
Compsognathus 22, 23
Corythosaurus 41
crested dinosaurs 28–29
Cretaceous Period 14–15
crocodilians 11, 12, 43
crows 27
Cryolophosaurus 29
Deinocheirus 45, 46
Deinonychus 49
diet and digestion 35
dinosaur types 8–9
Dinosauria 20, 21
Diplodocus
  necks and backbones 36–37, 39
  sauropod 27
  size 22
  tails 41
  teeth 35
dromaeosaurids 48, 49
Dryosaurus 40
dung *see* trace fossils
ears, dinosaur 30

EF

Edmontosaurus 15, 19, 35, 55
eggs 24, 58–59
Elasmosaurus 6–7
Eoraptor 25, 64
Epidexipteryx 22
Euparkeria 24
evolution 24–25, 46
eyes, dinosaur 31
family tree 64–65
feathers 7, 56–57
ferns 10, 13, 19
footprints 19, 52–53
fossils
  first finds 20–21
  footprints 52–53
  index 18
  molds and casts 19
  plants 19
  trace 19, 32

GH

Gallimimus 31
Gastornis 17
Gila monster 55
ginkgoes 10, 13
hadrosaurs 15, 34, 41, 55
herbivores *see* plant-eaters
herrerasaurids 64
Herrerasaurus 11
Heterodontosaurus 18, 35
hip bones 8
horned dinosaurs 14, 28–29, 34
  see also Triceratops
human skull and brain 27
Hylaeosaurus 21
Hyperodapedon 11
Hypsilophodon 51

IJKL

ichthyosaurs 7
Ichthyosaurus 13
Iguanodon 20, 23, 39
  foot bone 62
  hands 46
  teeth 35
index fossils 18
iridium 17
Jurassic Period 12–13,
Kentrosaurus 13, 43, 68
Lambeosaurus 29
Leaellynasaura 31
Lufengosaurus 60

MNO

Majungasaurus 6, 32
mammals 10, 15, 17, 55
maniraptoran 47, 48, 56, 58
Mantell, Gideon 20, 21
Mantell, Mary 20
Mantellisaurus 52
Marasuchus 64
marginocephalians 8, 64
marine reptiles 13, 15
mass extinction 16–17
meat-eaters 10, 32–33
Megalosaurus 20, 32, 66
Mei long 22
Mesozoic Era 7
Microraptor 7, 23
Miragaia 37
models of dinosaurs 21, 63
Monolophosaurus 7
Mosasaurus 15
museums 23, 62–63, 68–69
Neovenator 30
Nigersaurus 34
ornithischians 8, 57, 64
ornithomimids 51
ornithopods 8, 12, 14, 64
osteoderms 44, 54–55
Ouranosaurus 39, 45
Oviraptor 58
oviraptorosaur 40
oviraptorids 58
Owen, Richard 20–21

PQ

pachycephalosaurs 8, 29
Pachyrhinosaurus 28
paleontologists 18–19, 20
  dinosaur size calculations 22
  on excavations 60–61
  reconstruction of specimens 62–63
  see also individual names of paleontologists
Panderichthys 24
Pangaea 12
Parasaurolophus 29
placodonts 11
Placodus 11
plant-eaters 10–11, 34–35
plants 10, 13, 14, 19
Plateosaurus 11
plesiosaurs 7
Polacanthus 54
Proterosuchus 24
Protoceratops 59
Protosuchus 12
pseudosuchians 11
Psittacosaurus 35, 54–55, 64
Pterodactylus 12
pterosaurs 12
Quetzalcoatlus 15

RS

reproduction 24
rhynchosaurs 11
sails 44
salamanders 13
Saltasaurus 15, 54
saurischians 8, 39, 64
Sauropelta 14
sauropodomorphs 9, 64
sauropods 8, 12, 27
  arms and hands 46–47
  backbones 45
  claws 49
  Cretaceous Period 14, 15
  digestion 35
  fossil footprints 52
  jaws and teeth 34
  legs and feet 51
  necks 36–37
  size 22
  tails 42
scanning techniques 63
Scelidosaurus 12
Scolosaurus 38
sea reptiles 13, 15
Shunosaurus 43
Sinraptor 13
skulls and brains 26–27, 29
spinosaurids 32
Spinosaurus 39, 44
Stegoceras 29
stegosaurs 8, 12, 14, 37, 47
Stegosaurus 35, 44
Styracosaurus 14–15

T

tails 40–43
tetrapods 24
therizinosauroid 14
Therizinosaurus 48–49
theropods 8, 32
  brains 26
  Cretaceous Period 14
  diet 9, 33
  Early Jurassic 29
  family tree 64
  legs and feet 50–51
  and ornithischians 64
  plant-eating 48–49
  tyrannosauroid 12
  see also birds
thyreophorans 8, 64
Tianyulong confuciusi 57
titanosaur 47, 54
tongues, dinosaur 30
tools, paleontologist 60–61
trace fossils 19, 32
Triassic Period 10–11
Triceratops 23, 28–29, 49
types of dinosaurs 8–9
Tyrannosaurus
  legs 50
  limb bones 6
  necks 36–37
  sense of smell 30
  skeleton comparison 25
  skull and brain 27
  US fossil find 21
Tyrannosaurus rex
  arms and hands 47
  brains 27
  eyes 31
  jaws and teeth 33
  reconstruction 62–63
  theropod 9

VWXY

Velociraptor 36, 56
Vespersaurus 50
vision *see* eyes, dinosaur
volcanoes 16
warm-blooded dinosaurs 7
Williamsonia plants 13
Xing Xu, Dr 67
Yi qi 56
young dinosaurs 58–59

Acknowledgments

The publisher would like to thank the following people for their help with making the book: Camilla Hallinan for editorial guidance; Saloni Singh, Priyanka Sharma-Saddi, and Rakesh Sharma for the jacket; and Joanna Penning for proofreading and indexing.

The publisher would like to thank the following for their kind permission to reproduce their photographs:
(Key: a-above; b-below/bottom; c-center; l-left; r-right; t-top)

1 Dorling Kindersley: Staatliches Museum fur Naturkunde Stuttgart. **2 Dorling Kindersley:** Natural History Museum (tr); Natural History Museum, London (b). **Science Photo Library:** Max Alexander / B612 / Asteroid Day (cla). **4 Dorling Kindersley:** Courtesy of Dorset Dinosaur Museum (br); Natural History Museum (cl); Natural History Museum, London (bl). **Getty Images:** Peter Finch / Stone (tr). **5 Getty Images:** Mohamad Haghani / Stocktrek Images (tr). **6 Dorling Kindersley:** American Museum of Natural History (c). **6-7 Dreamstime.com:** Cornelius20 (b). **Fotolia:** Okea (cb). **7 Fotolia:** Okea (crb). **Getty Images:** Spencer Platt / Staff / Getty Images News (cla). **8-9 Dreamstime.com:** Mr1805 (c). **9 Dreamstime.com:** Hel080808 (br/Forest). **11 Dorling Kindersley:** James Kuether (bl); Natural History Museum, London (cla). **Dreamstime.com:** Corey A Ford (br). **12 Dorling Kindersley:** James Kuether (br). **13 Getty Images:** Kevin Schafer / The Image Bank (cr). **14-15 Science Photo Library:** James Kuether. **15 Max Bellomio:** (fbl). **Dorling Kindersley:** James Kuether (bl, fbr). **Science Photo Library:** James Kuether (cra); Michael Long (cb). **16-17 Alamy Stock Photo:** Allstar Picture Library Ltd. / DreamWorks. **16 Dreamstime.com:** Juliengrondin (tl). **17 Dorling Kindersley:** Jon Hughes (br). **NASA:** Goddard Space Flight Center Image by Reto Stöckli (land surface, shallow water, clouds) / MODIS (tl). **Science Photo Library:** Max Alexander / B612 / Asteroid Day (tr); Mark Pilkington / Geological Survey Of Canada (ca). **18 Alamy Stock Photo:** John Cancalosi (fcl, fclb); Robertharding / Nick Upton (fbl); Katewarn Images (ftl, fclb/limestone). **Dreamstime.com:** Salajean (fcla). **Getty Images / iStock:** Impalastock (clb). **Science Photo Library:** Patrick Dumas / Look At Sciences (cl). **19 Alamy Stock Photo:** Jill Stephenson (tl). **Dorling Kindersley:** Trustees of the National Museums Of Scotland (cr); The American Museum of Natural History (tr). **20 Alamy Stock Photo:** The Natural History Museum (tl). **Dorling Kindersley:** Natural History Museum, London (cla). **20-21 Alamy Stock Photo:** The Natural History Museum (c). **Dorling Kindersley:** Natural History Museum, London (b). **21 Alamy Stock Photo:** Bilwissedition Ltd. & Co. Kg (tl); Adrian Chinery (ca). **Getty Images:** Bettmann (crb). **22 Science Photo Library:** Philippe Psaila (tr). **23 Dorling Kindersley:** American Museum of Natural History (tl); James Kuether (cra). **24 Dorling Kindersley:** The Oxford University Museum of Natural History (cla); Jon Hughes (clb, crb). **24-25 Dorling Kindersley:** Senckenberg Gesellschaft Fuer Naturforschung Museum (t). **25 Dorling Kindersley:** Geoff Brightling / ESPL - modelmaker / ESPL (tr). **Dreamstime.com:** Christopher Meder (b). **26 Dorling Kindersley:** Royal Tyrrell Museum of Palaeontology, Alberta, Canada (c). **Science Photo Library:** Millard H. Sharp (br). **26-27 Alamy Stock Photo:** Martin Shields. **27 Dreamstime.com:** David Havel (bl). **Getty Images / iStock:** Warpaintcobra (crb). **28 Alamy Stock Photo:** DM7 (tl). **28-29 Alamy Stock Photo:** Steppenwolf. **29 Alamy Stock Photo:** Stocktrek Images, Inc. / Walter Myers (crb). **Dorling Kindersley:** James Kuether (tr); Royal Tyrrell Museum of Palaeontology, Alberta, Canada (cr). **30 Alamy Stock Photo:** Stocktrek Images, Inc. / Sergey Krasovskiy (cl). **Dorling Kindersley:** James Kuether (crb). **Shutterstock.com:** Nneirda (bl). **31 Dorling Kindersley:** James Kuether (c). **32 Dorling Kindersley:** Natural History Museum, London (tl, c). Image courtesy of the Royal Saskatchewan Museum: (cla). **32-33 Dorling Kindersley:** James Kuether. **33 Dorling Kindersley:** Staatliches Museum fur Naturkunde Stuttgart (tl). **34-35 Science Photo Library:** James Kuether. **34 Alamy Stock Photo:** The Natural History Museum (br). **Dorling Kindersley:** Natural History Museum, London (ftr, tr). **Getty Images:** The Washington Post (bl). **35 Dorling Kindersley:** Carnegie Museum of Natural History, Pittsburgh (cla); Natural History Museum, London (cra, tc). **36 Getty Images:** Murat Taner / The Image Bank (cla). **36-37 Dorling Kindersley:** Senckenberg Gesellschaft Fuer Naturforschung Museum (t). **Dreamstime.com:** Corey A Ford (b). **37 Alamy Stock Photo:** Dpa Picture Alliance (cl). **38-39 Dorling Kindersley:** Senckenberg Gesellschaft Fuer Naturforschung Museum. **38 Alamy Stock Photo:** The Natural History Museum (cla). **39 Dorling Kindersley:** Natural History Museum, London (tr). **National Science Foundation, USA:** Zina Deretsky (br). **40-41 Dorling Kindersley:** Senckenberg Gesellschaft Fuer Naturforschung Museum (c). **40 Acta Palaeontologica Polonica is published by Institute of Paleobiology, Polish Academy of Sciences:** Rinchen Barsbold, Halszka Osmólska, Mahito Watabe, Philip J. Currie, and Khishigjaw Tsogtbaatar / Acta Palaeontologica Polonica 45 (2), 2000: 97-106 (bl). **Dorling Kindersley:** James Kuether (b). **41 Dorling Kindersley:** American Museum of Natural History (t). **42 Louie Psihoyos ©psihoyos.com. 42-43 Dorling Kindersley:** James Kuether (b). **43 Alamy Stock Photo:** Stocktrek Images, Inc. / Mohamad Haghani (t). **Dorling Kindersley:** Royal Tyrrell Museum of Palaeontology, Alberta, Canada (bc). **44 Science Photo Library:** James Kuether (cl). **44-45 Dorling Kindersley:** Senckenberg Nature Museum, Frankfurt. **45 Getty Images:** MediaNews Group / Boulder Daily Camera via Getty Images / Contributor (cr). **Science Photo Library:** Mark P. Witton (tl). **Shutterstock.com:** Danny Ye (cra). **46 Dorling Kindersley:** Natural History Museum (bl). **Louie Psihoyos ©psihoyos.com:** (tl). **Science Photo Library:** James Kuether (clb, clb/Deinocheirus). **47 Alamy Stock Photo:** Dpa Picture Alliance / Jordan Raza / ZB (bc). **Dorling Kindersley:** Senckenberg Gesellschaft Fuer Naturforschung Museum (tc). **Dreamstime.com:** Leonello Calvetti (c). **Getty Images:** Universal History Archive / Universal Images Group (tl). **Science Photo Library:** Millard H. Sharp / Science Source (tr). **48-49 Dorling Kindersley:** Natural History Museum, London. **49 Alamy Stock Photo:** The Natural History Museum (cla). **Dorling Kindersley:** Natural History Museum, London (cb, bl); Peabody Museum of Natural History, Yale University (br). Dr. Octávio Mateus: (tr). **50 Getty Images:** Mohamad Haghani / Stocktrek Images (br). **© 2021 Springer Nature Limited:** Langer, M.C., Martins, N.d.O., Manzig, P.C. et al. A new desert-dwelling dinosaur (Theropoda, Noasaurinae) from the Cretaceous of south Brazil. Sci Rep 9, 9379 (2019). https://doi.org/10.1038/s41598-019-45306-9 (bl). **51 Dorling Kindersley:** The Natural History Museum / Alamy Stock Photo (bc); Royal Tyrrell Museum of Palaeontology, Alberta, Canada (cr); Natural History Museum, London (br). **52 Dorling Kindersley:** Natural History Museum, London (bl). **Getty Images:** Alexander Koerner / Contributor (c). **52-53 Alamy Stock Photo:** Tom Bean. **53 Dorling Kindersley:** Natural History Museum, London (tl). **54 Dorling Kindersley:** Museo Argentino De Cirendas Naterales, Buenos Aires (tl); Natural History Museum (bl). **54-55 Dorling Kindersley:** Senckenberg Gesellschaft Fuer Naturforschung Museum. **55 Alamy Stock Photo:** The Natural History Museum (br). **Dorling Kindersley:** Natural History Museum, London (tl); Jerry Young (bl). **Getty Images:** Peter Finch / Stone (tr). **56 Alamy Stock Photo:** Mohamad Haghani (bl); Martin Shields (crb). **57 Alamy Stock Photo:** Martin Shields (cra); Stocktrek Images, Inc. / Roman Garcia Mora (bc). **Dorling Kindersley:** Natural History Museum, London (br). **58-59 Louie Psihoyos ©psihoyos.com. 58 Alamy Stock Photo:** Dpa Picture Alliance / Holger Hollemann (bl). **Dorling Kindersley:** Courtesy of Dorset Dinosaur Museum (c). **Science Photo Library:** Millard H. Sharp / Science Source (br). **59 Dorling Kindersley:** American Museum of Natural History (r). **Getty Images:** Mark Boster / Los Angeles Times (tr). **60 Ardea:** Francois Gohier (cla). **Shutterstock.com:** Sipa (cra). **60-61 Dorling Kindersley:** Natural History Museum, London (tools). **61 Mary Evans Picture Library:** Natural History Museum (tc). **Science Photo Library:** Natural History Museum, London (tl, tr). **62 Dorling Kindersley:** Natural History Museum, London (cra). **Louie Psihoyos ©psihoyos.com:** (cl). **62-63 123RF.com:** Ian Dikhtiar. **63 Dorling Kindersley:** Natural History Museum, London (tr). **Science Photo Library:** Patrick Dumas / Look At Sciences (crb); Pascal Goetgheluck (tl); Philippe Psaila (cr). **64 Dorling Kindersley:** James Kuether (cl, c). **66 Getty Images:** John B. Carnett / Bonnier Corporation / Popular Science (br). **67 Alamy Stock Photo:** Lou Linwei (c). **Getty Images:** Karl Gehring / The Denver Post (tl). **68 FLPA:** Derek Hall (cla). **Getty Images:** Ulrich Baumgarten (clb); Jeff Swensen (bl). **Science Photo Library:** James L. Amos (r). **69 Getty Images:** MediaNews Group / Boston Herald (bl). **Shutterstock.com:** Universal Pictures / Kobal (crb). **71 123RF.com:** Mark Turner (br)

All other images © Dorling Kindersley
For further information see: **www.dkimages.com**